HOW DO I GET THROUGH THIS?

Pressing On When You Want To Turn Back,
Give Up or Walk Away

Written by:
Kelley Brown, Marissa Henley, Katy McCown, Bronwyn Cardwell, Wendy Blight

With contributions from:
Quantrilla Ard, Melanie Porter, Bethany Ruth, Joy Williams and the First 5 Team

We must exchange whispers with God before shouts with the world.

LYSA TERKEURST

Pair your Study Guide with the First 5 mobile app!

This Study Guide is designed to accompany your study of Scripture in the First 5 mobile app. You can use it as a standalone study, or as an accompanying guide to the daily content within First 5.

First 5 is a free mobile app developed by Proverbs 31 Ministries to transform your daily time with God.

HI FRIEND!

If you've ever trained for a marathon, you're familiar with the dreaded possibility of "hitting the wall"— a period during a race when the runner's physical and mental strength are so depleted that continuing on feels impossible.

Maybe you've experienced similar feelings of fatigue and defeat in a demanding job, a broken relationship, debt-ridden finances or sinful habits you're desperate to break. Maybe this very moment, you can't decide which direction to head or whether the risk is worth taking. Suddenly it seems much easier to just turn back, give up, or walk away. In these moments, we fool ourselves into believing that everything will be better if we just have comfort and control.

In Exodus, God reveals a better way: a way that tests our faith and requires our trust but ultimately brings us through the wilderness and into the promised land where God's best awaits us. Better yet, we experience the most remarkable blessing of all: God's presence. He longs to dwell with His beloved people — that includes you and me! Will we choose to make our home with Him?

You might feel as stuck and hopeless as the Israelites enslaved in Egypt, but our journey through this second book of the Old Testament will teach us some key lessons in faith and trust as we navigate our own seasons in the wilderness. The book of Exodus is filled with testimonies of hope and success involving people who trusted God to lead them out of distress and into freedom.

Our journey with the Israelites won't always be easy. We'll witness slavery, murder, plagues and blatant disobedience. More than once, you might find yourself screaming at the pages: "Don't do it!" There are some cringe-worthy moments for sure. But you certainly won't be bored! The wonders of God far outweigh the recklessness of His people.

As Exodus closes, the Israelites are watching for God's cloud to lift as a sign to pack up and continue moving toward the promised land. Day by day, they're learning to trust and follow Yahweh. As we journey together through this study, we will too. Let's get going!

Walking alongside you,

Kelley Brown, Marissa Henley, Katy McCown, Bronwyn Cardwell, Wendy Blight
Your Exodus Study Guide Writing Team

INTRODUCING
EXODUS

Exodus is the second of the first five books of the Bible. This collection (Genesis, Exodus, Leviticus, Numbers and Deuteronomy) is traditionally referred to as the Pentateuch, the Torah or the "Law of Moses." Pentateuch comes from two Greek words which translate as "five scrolls." Collectively, they document the early history of God's chosen people, their covenant relationship, the forming of a nation through deliverance, and instructions for holy living. In short, the Pentateuch is all about God teaching His people how to live faithfully as He unfolds His plan of salvation ... a plan to bring fallen humanity back into fellowship with a holy God.

The English title of the book comes from the Greek noun *exodos* used in the Septuagint, an early Greek translation of the Old Testament that was made in Egypt during the third century before Christ. *Exodos* means "a going out," "exit" or "departure." It's certainly a logical and appropriate title since the primary storyline is Israel's divinely orchestrated departure from Egypt.

It's also a fitting description of the Israelites' behavior post-Egypt ... the newly freed nation repeatedly departed from the path of obedience, holy living and true worship.

Exodus continues the story from Genesis to chronicle the early history of the Hebrew people in Egypt, covering a span of about 85 years. [1] The book documents events from the Israelites' enslavement and the birth of Moses to the completion and dedication of the tabernacle and God's presence filling it with His glory.

In the simplest breakdown of Exodus, the first half (Chapters 1-18) records God's deliverance of the Israelites from Egypt, and the second half (Chapters 19-40) covers God's covenant with the Israelites at the foot of Mount Sinai. The heart of the book, however, is God making Himself known (to the Israelites and the Egyptians) and providing a way to dwell in the midst of His beloved people.

WHY EXPERIENCE EXODUS?

Exodus might be one of the most intriguing and unpredictable books of the Bible! Who could guess that the Hebrew baby boy who narrowly escaped death would've grown up as a prince in Pharaoh's palace, rashly murdered an abusive Egyptian, fled the country and bided his time as a shepherd, and then at the ripe old age of 80, reluctantly accepted what seemed like an impossible mission from God? This man named Moses was being asked to confront the king of the ancient world's greatest superpower and lead tens of thousands of Hebrew slaves out of Egypt and into the promised land. And that's just the first few chapters of the book!

Without a doubt, Exodus is an epic adventure story. But let's be honest ... we don't open our Bibles to be entertained. We come to the pages of Scripture in search of truth, clarity, instruction and assurance. We come hoping to learn a little more about the mighty God we love and serve.

Exodus offers all of this and more.

It helps us understand who God is and what He asks of us as His chosen people. It unveils rituals, feasts, laws and requirements that become an essential part of the Israelites' worship and faith until the coming of Christ. It also reminds us why the world so desperately needs a Savior. And why we can face the future with confident faith when we actually feel like giving up.

DISCOVER GOD'S HEART

Through the eyes of Moses, a man who knew God face-to-face, we will experience revelations of Yahweh's character and nature as He faithfully preserves Abraham's line and establishes Israel as a nation. We will observe a God who keeps His promises, who hears our cries, sees our circumstances, and intervenes when necessary.

Exodus reveals a God who performs miracles, parts seas, quenches thirst, satisfies hunger, sustains the weary and longs to make His home with His people. In the words of Moses, He is *"majestic in holiness, awesome in glorious deeds, doing wonders"* (Exodus 15:11). And at the same time, He is patient, *"merciful and gracious, slow to anger, and abounding in steadfast love and faithfulness"* (Exodus 34:6). How much easier it is to confront our fears and trials with confident faith when we know and can trust the heart of God!

EXAMINE OUR HEARTS

Our own hearts are frequently the greatest obstacle to obedience. It's tempting to criticize the delivered Israelites for their grumblings and fickle faith. But as we journey through the book of Exodus, I challenge us to look inward and examine our own wayward spirit.

Have you ever driven somewhere and realized you have no memory of how you got there? Your eyes were on the road, but your focus was somewhere else. Like the Israelites in the wilderness, we can follow after God yet have distracted minds and discontented hearts. Exodus will show us the importance of remembering God's faithfulness in the past and keeping Him at the forefront as we move forward. The Ten Commandments and guidelines for holy living are helpful in revealing whether our hearts are aligned with His. Moses figured out early on in his ministry that a humble and grateful heart leads to an obedient faith. And obedience invites God's favor and blessing: Jesus Himself said, *"Blessed rather are those who hear the word of God and keep it"* (Luke 11:28).

REMEMBER OUR HOPE

Every believer goes through seasons in the desert. Maybe opening your Bible right now is a struggle. You feel stagnant in your faith journey. Or maybe you feel stuck in unhealthy, even destructive patterns. Exodus reminds us that God never intended for His people to remain trapped in their sin or sufferings. The Israelites' deliverance from slavery was a foretaste of the freedom and victory Jesus secured for all believers.

Embrace His promises! Rest in Moses' declaration: *"The Lord will fight for you; you need only to be still"* (Exodus 14:14, NIV). The God of Israel, the same God we worship and serve today, set His heart on you before the beginning of time. And even when unbelief, doubts or sin lead you astray, God pursues you with a love that won't let go.

WHO WROTE EXODUS?

The book of Exodus doesn't explicitly identify the author, but most Bible scholars credit Moses. He is believed to have also written the other four books of the Pentateuch: Genesis, Leviticus, Numbers and Deuteronomy.

Moses obviously wasn't present at creation or the events before his lifetime, but the stories in Genesis would have been preserved and passed down from generation to generation until Moses, through divine inspiration, recorded them. There are portions of the Pentateuch that seem to have been added by a different writer (How ironic would it be for Moses to document his own humility in Numbers 12:3?) and at a later date (particularly the details of Moses' death and burial in Deuteronomy 34.) But since we know that all Scripture is God-breathed, we can rest assured that the Holy Spirit guided any editing of the Pentateuch, and every verse of Scripture has importance, regardless of whose human hand penned the words. (2 Timothy 3:16)

Here is some evidence that supports Moses as the author of Exodus: Exodus opens with a list of names and details that connect with the story recorded at the end of Genesis. Since all five books of the Pentateuch reflect similar genre and content with the storyline flowing seamlessly from book to book, and because Moses is widely believed to be the author of those records, it can be concluded that he also wrote Exodus.

Throughout the book of Exodus, there are several references to Moses writing or being commanded to write. (Exodus 17:14; 24:4; 34:27)

The book provides accurate details regarding Egyptian religion and culture, leading historians to conclude that it could only have been written by someone well-versed in their customs and traditions. Having grown up as Egyptian royalty, Moses would have been well-educated in these areas. Acts 7:22 affirms this assumption: *"And Moses was instructed in all the wisdom of the Egyptians, and he was mighty in his words and deeds."*

When Jesus quoted from Exodus in Mark 7:10 and 12:26, He attributed the words to Moses. This is probably the most compelling evidence of all!

God said to Moses,

"I AM WHO I AM."

And he said,

"Say this to the

people of Israel:

'I AM has sent me to you.'"

EXODUS 3:14

THE 3 STAGES
OF MOSES' LIFE

AGES
0-40

EGYPT
Exodus 2:11
Acts 7:23

AGES
41-80

MIDIAN
Exodus 2:15
Acts 7:20-30

AGES
81-120

THE WILDERNESS
Deuteronomy 29:5; 31:2; 34:7

GETTING TO KNOW THE AUTHOR

"And there has not arisen a prophet since in Israel like Moses, whom the Lord knew face to face, none like him for all the signs and the wonders that the Lord sent him to do in the land of Egypt, to Pharaoh and to all his servants and to all his land, and for all the mighty power and all the great deeds of terror that Moses did in the sight of all Israel" (Deuteronomy 34:10-12).

Moses is one of the most well-known and esteemed figures in biblical history. His life and ministry are covered in the books of Exodus through Deuteronomy, but we learn the most about his birth, upbringing and call to ministry in the book of Exodus. As a man whom *"the Lord knew face to face,"* he served as a precursor to Jesus through his roles as God's chosen deliverer, prophet, lawgiver and mediator (Deuteronomy 34:10). It was through Moses that God would reveal His purposes for Israel and sustain the covenant relationship He had initiated with Abraham centuries before.

While his accomplishments were many, Moses is best remembered for leading the Israelites out of Egypt and receiving the Ten Commandments from God at Mount Sinai. For a leader with such authority, it's surprising and impressive to see him described in Numbers 12:3 as the most humble man *"on the face of the earth."* When he died in Moab at 120 years old, he was secretly buried by none other than God Himself. (Deuteronomy 34:6)

What an honor! His legacy is so great that his name appears in 19 Old Testament books and 12 New Testament books, most notably in Acts and Hebrews. We also read about his appearance with Elijah and Jesus during the transfiguration account in Matthew 17:1-8. Exodus particularly highlights Moses' servant leadership and obedient faith to carry out the Lord's instructions. (Exodus 40:16) But contrary to what you may have concluded, he was far from perfect. God didn't select Moses because he was confident, eloquent, strategic or particularly bold. The Hebrew man had insecurities, doubts and lapses in judgment just like all of us. He had committed murder, was reluctant to accept his commission from God and feared public speaking. He would even make a mistake so significant that it cost him entry into the promised land. God chose Moses because He delights in using ordinary people to do extraordinary work!

I love how God takes our concerns into account. He faithfully provided Moses with everything he needed to accomplish his mission, including a spokesperson — Moses' brother, Aaron! Moses' humble response was to remain prayerful, (Exodus 32-34) obedient (Exodus 40:16) and teachable (Exodus 18:24; 33:13) over the span of his work and ministry. In response, God continued to grant Moses favor and responsibility. Ultimately, Moses' life and ministry as Israel's redeemer pointed to One who would bring everlasting deliverance for all people and all nations. (Hebrews 3:1-6)

THE BIG PICTURE

The book of Exodus continues the historical narrative in Genesis, which recorded how the patriarch Jacob and his family came to reside in Egypt's land of Goshen. As you may recall from Genesis 37-47, Jacob's sons had sold their brother (the favorite child) to some traveling Midianite traders. Those men took Joseph with them to Egypt, where he unexpectedly rose to power and influence through divine favor with Pharaoh. Meanwhile, a famine in his homeland of Canaan led Jacob to send his sons to Egypt to find more grain. A surprise encounter with their brother (the newly appointed ruler over the land!) eventually led to forgiveness, a family reunion, and the move of Jacob's descendants to the prospering nation.

It's at this point in the story that Exodus picks up and continues the account from Genesis. In the 400 years since the family's migration, Jacob's 70 descendants had grown immensely in population but gradually lost the freedom and favor they once enjoyed during Joseph's reign as second in command. A newly crowned Egyptian king saw their ever-increasing multitude as a threat and tried to gain control by brutally enslaving them. That was just the beginning of his tyranny. His evil edicts escalated until an order to drown all Hebrew baby boys threatened to diminish God's chosen people.

All along, God was watching over the plight of His people until it was time to intervene. Remembering His covenant with the patriarchs to make Abraham's descendants into a great nation and extend their blessing, God activated a rescue plan through His chosen leader, mediator and deliverer — Moses. (Genesis 17:1-8)

God had big plans for the Israelites once they left Egypt ... He would confirm His covenant relationship and make them into *"a kingdom of priests and a holy nation"* (Exodus 19:6). They would construct a tabernacle so God could make His home with them. And eventually Israel would bring the blessings of Abraham and his family to the entire world. (Genesis 12:3) But first ... they would have to learn how to be faithful.

PATRIARCHS

Patriarch is a term that generally means "father" or "head of a family." Sometimes it even indicates the founder of a family line, group or tribe.

In the Bible, the term most often refers to Abraham, his son, Isaac, and Isaac's son, Jacob, who were the forefathers of the Israelites, and therefore founders of the nation and of God's chosen people. "Abraham the patriarch" is mentioned in Hebrews 7:4, and he was the one with whom God established a covenant to multiply his descendants and extend His divine blessing to all the earth through his family line. (Genesis 12:1-3).

The 12 sons of Jacob are also sometimes referred to as patriarchs because it was from them that the 12 tribes of Israel descended. (Acts 7:8-9) Recorded in the book of Genesis, the 12 brothers were Reuben, Simeon, Levi, Judah, Issachar, Zebulun, Joseph, Benjamin, Dan, Naphtali, Gad and Asher. Jesus descended from the tribe of Judah. (Matthew 1:1-16)

COMMUNITY AND CULTURE

HISTORICAL AND CULTURAL CONTEXT

Bible scholars generally fall into one of two camps when speculating about the date of the Exodus from Egypt: the Early Date Theory (1446 B.C.) or the Late Date Theory (1290 B.C.) [2] There are various reasons for the difficulty in precisely identifying the time period, but one of the main factors is the lack of names in reference to the Egyptian pharaohs. Thankfully, even without exact knowledge of the date, Exodus' message remains clear. Themes of oppression, deliverance, rebellion, worship, holy living and God's presence transcend time and cultural differences, making Exodus an eternally relevant story.

During the proposed time frame of Exodus (between 1500-1200 B.C.), Egypt was at the height of civilization. It reigned as the wealthiest and most powerful land in the Ancient Near East, surpassing all other nations in the fields of medicine, architecture, literature and military strength.

The Nile River was a central part of Egypt's identity and provided water, food, transportation and irrigation for the country. Based on their own creation account, Egypt and all of its life had sprung forth from this river. In fact, Greek historian Herodotus famously called Egypt "the gift of the Nile."[3] They continued to see the river as their primary source for existence, particularly because it was linked to their god of fertility, Hapi.[4]

Egyptian religion involved worship of many different gods and goddesses. When we study the ten plagues, we'll learn how each plague was directed by God to attack a particular false deity in addition to Pharaoh and the Egyptian people. Even the miracles Moses was equipped to perform were directed to prove God's supreme power over the culture's sorcerers and dark magic.

UNIQUELY EXODUS

Perhaps more than any other book in the Old Testament, Exodus helps us understand God's overall plan of redemption. Let's back up to Genesis to set the stage for all that God would introduce in Exodus.

In the garden of Eden, Adam and Eve were given a special commission as image-bearers of God. Their job was *"to 'fill the earth' with reflections of God's glory"* (Genesis 1:28). [5] But in one moment of distrust, that all changed. Creation now faced a dilemma ... how can fallen humanity stand in the presence of a holy God? Adam and Eve's sin required them to be exiled from the garden and from God's presence. Because they were no longer perfect reflections of the Lord, sin would fill the earth as humanity multiplied.

Fortunately, God had a plan. He initiated a covenant with Abraham to restore His blessing that had been blocked by Adam and Eve's sin. Through Abraham's descendants, God would create a great nation through which all people on earth would be blessed. (Genesis 12:3)

Yet, for all of humanity to fulfill our mission in this world — the mission of multiplying and magnifying God's glory throughout creation — the problem of sin had to be resolved. One biblical scholar explained it this way: "The book of Genesis showed the plight of the human race and its need for salvation. The call of Abraham began the process of divine rescue. Then Jacob's migration to Egypt seemed to put the plan aside. But in a most dramatic fashion, Exodus shows the divine plan reactivated." [6] Nothing — not oppression, unbelief, rebellion or idolatry — could hinder God's ability to accomplish His purpose for His people.

Exodus enters God's story as a critical piece of the puzzle and the key to understanding the cross of Christ. It's in Exodus that God introduced the need for:

A Chosen Deliverer
A Mediator
A Prophet
A Lawgiver
A Holy Priest
The Atoning Blood of a Spotless Lamb

For the first time in biblical history, God instituted the Passover, miraculously produced manna, issued the Law, delivered instructions for a tabernacle, set up a sacrificial system to atone for sins, and came down to dwell in the midst of His people. The Exodus story uniquely details how God prepared the way for salvation so the garden of Eden would not just be restored but also expanded to all of creation.

Without all these elements of the Exodus story, we could not fully grasp the significance of who Jesus is and what He came to do on our behalf.

Without understanding God's desire to dwell among us, we can't fathom why He would go to such great lengths to reconcile a sinful race to Himself. Or why Jesus would leave the heavenly realms to become flesh and walk this earth in human form.

Without discovering Israel's identity as God's treasured possession and a nation to represent God to the rest of the world, we miss the significance of carrying out that same mission in the world today. (Exodus 19:5; Matthew 28:18-20) As the Apostle Peter declared, *"But you are a chosen race, a royal priesthood, a holy nation, a people for his own possession, that you may proclaim the excellencies of him who called you out of darkness into his marvelous light"* (1 Peter 2:9).

CONNECTING EXODUS TO THE REST OF SCRIPTURE

While Exodus could stand alone as a great adventure story, it's part of a larger and grander narrative that spans both the Old and New Testaments. The book records Israel's deliverance from Egypt, which is the defining redemptive event of the Old Testament. It's a picture of the gospel; a model for salvation that we watch unfold in the gospel accounts.

We think of salvation as a New Testament theme. But the concept of salvation didn't start with the cross, or even with Jesus' birth. It began in Genesis with God's promise to restore His relationship with humanity. When we place the Exodus story in the grand scheme of God's plan, we're reminded that His purpose in the Israelites' rescue went beyond deliverance from slavery and salvation of Abraham's line. Yahweh desired the community He had once enjoyed in the garden with Adam and Eve. He longed to lead the Israelites to a fruitful land where they could learn how to live as His chosen people and enjoy His divine presence.

The heart of God is the same today as it was in Moses' lifetime. Jesus' death and resurrection accomplished more than our deliverance from the bondage of sin. Because of our Savior, we can experience abundant life here on earth and have permanent and unhindered access to the Lord's presence! Theology professor Michael Horton notes that God dwelling in the midst of His people "is the heart of God's covenantal purposes from Genesis to Revelation." [7]

Here are some of the themes of Exodus that carry through into the New Testament and find fulfillment and completion in Jesus Christ.

COVENANT
Old Covenant: Exodus 24
New Covenant: Hebrews 8:6-13

REMEMBRANCE
The Passover: Exodus 12:1-30
The Lord's Supper: Luke 22:7-20

SACRIFICES
Animal Sacrifices as a Sin Offering: Exodus 29:36
Christ's Sacrifice as the Final Offering: Hebrews 10:1-18

BLOOD OF A LAMB
The Passover Lamb: Exodus 12:3-5
The Lamb of God: Revelation 7:10, 14

DELIVERANCE
Deliverance from Slavery: Exodus 20:2
Deliverance from Sin: Romans 6:14-19

PROVISION OF FOOD
Manna and Quail: Exodus 16
Fish and Loaves; Bread of Life: John 6:1-13, 35

INTERCESSOR
Moses Pleads on Israel's Behalf: Exodus 32:11-14
Jesus Pleads on Our Behalf: Romans 8:34; Hebrews 7:25

THE LAW
Humanity Can't Uphold the Law: Exodus 20:1-23:13
Jesus Satisfied the Law's Requirements: Matthew 5:17-20

TABERNACLE, TEMPLE
A Physical Building: Exodus 25:8
Our Bodies as a Temple: 1 Corinthians 3:16, 6:19

GOD'S PRESENCE
With Moses: Exodus 3:12
In Us: John 14:16-17

PRIESTHOOD
Priests Must be Consecrated: Exodus 29
Jesus Has a Permanent Priesthood: Romans 7:24-28

EXODUS
AT A GLANCE

AUTHOR: Moses

SETTING: Exodus predominantly follows the nation of Israel in three geographical locations ...
Egypt (1:1-13:16)
Wilderness (13:17-18:27)
Sinai (19:1-40:38)

TIME PERIOD:
The Late Bronze Age
(between 1550-1200 B.C.)

GENRE: Historical Narrative

PURPOSE:
God faithfully delivers the Israelites out of slavery in Egypt to take possession of the promised land as a fulfillment of His covenant with the patriarchs to make Abraham's descendants into a great nation.

KEY CHARACTERS:
God ("Yahweh"), Pharaoh, Pharaoh's daughter, Miriam, Moses, Aaron, Joshua, Jethro, Bezalel, Oholiab

KEY PLACES: Egypt, the Nile River, Midian, the Red Sea, the wilderness, Mount Sinai, the promised land (Canaan)

KEY VERSES: Exodus 19:4-6
"'You yourselves have seen what I did to the Egyptians, and how I bore you on eagles' wings and brought you to myself. Now therefore, if you will indeed obey my voice and keep my covenant, you shall be my treasured possession among all peoples, for all the earth is mine; and you shall be to me a kingdom of priests and a holy nation.' These are the words that you shall speak to the people of Israel."

KEY THEMES: God's covenant promise, deliverance, obedience, holy living, God's presence

KEY EVENTS

ISRAELITES ENSLAVED IN EGYPT
Exodus 1

MOSES' CALLING AT THE BURNING BUSH
Exodus 3-4

THE 10 PLAGUES
Exodus 7:14-13:16

THE PASSOVER
Exodus 12

CROSSING THE RED SEA
Exodus 13:17-14:31

THE SONG OF MOSES
Exodus 15:1-21

JOSHUA DEFEATS THE AMALEKITES
Exodus 17:8-16

THE TEN COMMANDMENTS
Exodus 20:1-17

GOD INVITES ISRAEL INTO A COVENANT RELATIONSHIP
Exodus 24

THE GOLDEN CALF
Exodus 32

GOD'S GLORY FILLS THE TABERNACLE
Exodus 40:34-38

MAJOR MOMENTS IN EXODUS

WEEK 1
Exodus 1-2 — Pharaoh oppressed the Israelites, but God heard their cries for help.
Exodus 3:1-12 — God called Moses to deliver the Israelites out of Egypt.
Exodus 3:13-15 — God revealed His name — Yahweh — to Moses.
Exodus 3:16-22 — God promised to bring the Israelites out of slavery in Egypt and into the promised land.
Exodus 4:1-9 — God gave three miraculous signs to authenticate Moses' testimony and instructions to the Israelites.

WEEK 2
Exodus 4:10-18 — Moses protested but was assured by God.
Exodus 4:19-31 — Moses returned to Egypt.
Exodus 5:1-14 — Moses told Pharaoh to let the people go.
Exodus 5:15-21 — The people complained that Moses made things worse.
Exodus 5:22-6:12 — Moses complained to God.

WEEK 3
Exodus 6:13-27 — The genealogy of Moses and Aaron were recorded.
Exodus 6:28-7:13 — Moses and Aaron performed the first sign before Pharaoh.
Exodus 7:14-8:32 — God sent plagues of blood, frogs, gnats and flies.
Exodus 9:1-10:20 — God sent plagues of disease, boils, hail and locusts.
Exodus 10:21-29 — God sent a plague of darkness.

WEEK 4
Exodus 11:1-12:28 — The final plague is revealed, and God gave instructions for the Passover.
Exodus 12:29-13:16 — The death of Egypt's firstborn and the consecration of Israel's firstborn were recorded.
Exodus 13:17-14:31 — The Israelites crossed the Red Sea.
Exodus 15 — Moses and the people sang a song, and bitter water was made sweet.
Exodus 16:1-17:7 — Despite the Israelites' grumbling, God sent bread from heaven and water from the rock.

WEEK 5

Exodus 17:8-18:27 — Israel defeated Amalek, and Jethro gave his advice.

Exodus 19 — The Israelites set up camp at Mt. Sinai.

Exodus 20:1-17 — God gave the Ten Commandments to His people.

Exodus 20:18-21 — The people were afraid of God's presence.

Exodus 20:22-,23:19 — God revealed the details of the law and ordained three feasts.

WEEK 6

Exodus 23:20-24:18 — Canaan was promised, and the covenant was confirmed.

Exodus 25:1-31:18 — Many laws for worship were given.

Exodus 32:1-14 — The people worshipped a golden calf.

Exodus 32:15-35 — Moses interceded, and God still sent a plague.

Exodus 33:1-11 — The Israelites mourned with repentance, and God met with Moses.

WEEK 7

Exodus 33:12-34:28 — God through Moses wrote the Ten Commandments again.

Exodus 34:29-35 — The face of Moses shone brightly.

Exodus 35:1-3 — Moses repeated the regulations about the Sabbath day.

Exodus 35:4-29 — Moses gave instructions regarding offerings.

Exodus 35:30-36:7 — Moses instructed the people on who was to build the tabernacle.

WEEK 8

Exodus 36:8-38 — The tabernacle was constructed.

Exodus 37:1-9 — God revealed the design of the veil and the ark.

Exodus 37:10-29 — God revealed the design of the Holy Place and its contents.

Exodus 38 — God revealed the design of the outer courtyard and its contents.

Exodus 39-40 — The priestly garments were created and God's glory fell upon the tabernacle.

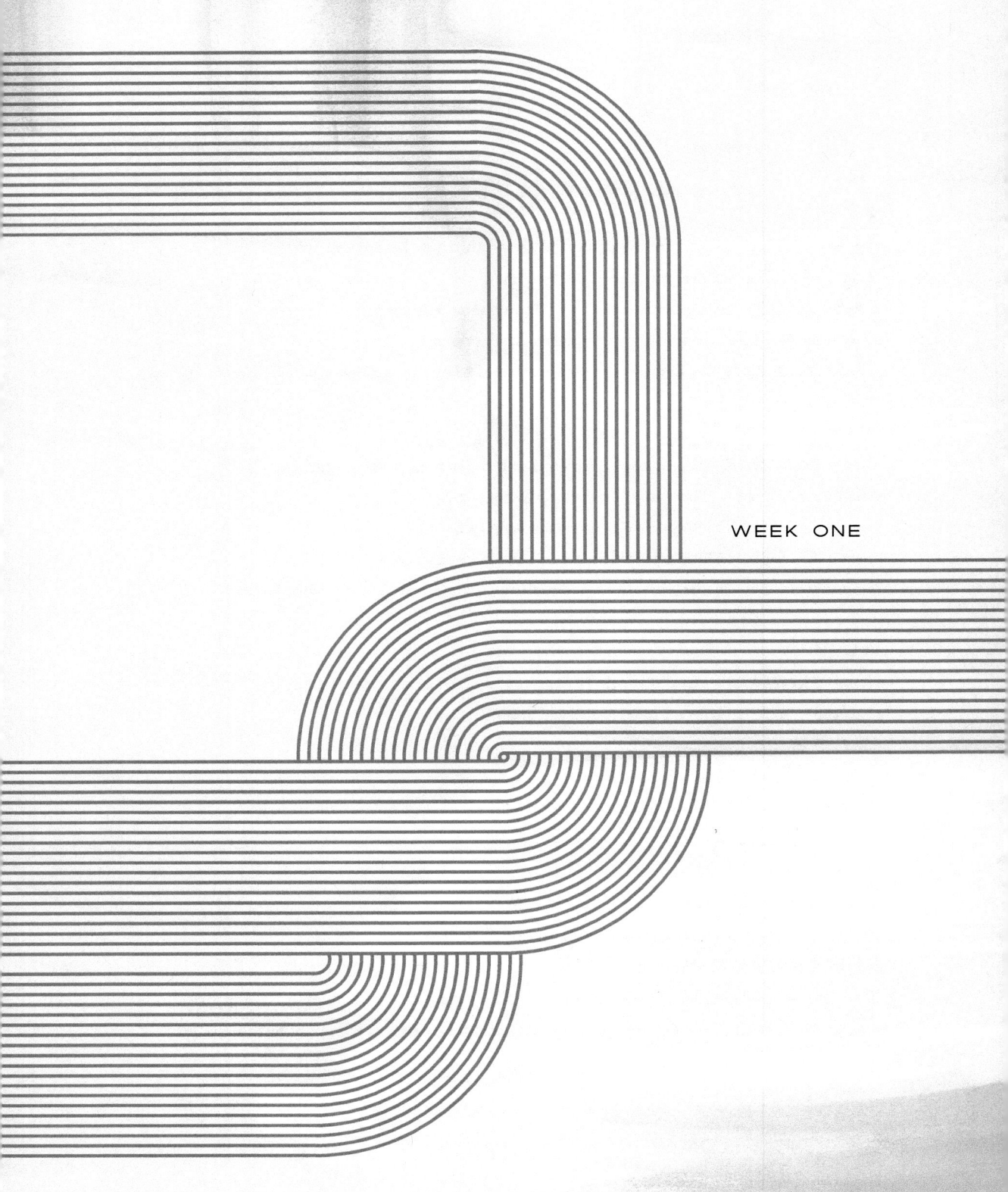

DAY one

SCRIPTURE READING: Exodus 1-2

MAJOR MOMENT: Pharaoh oppressed the Israelites, but God heard their cries for help.

The book of Exodus begins right where Genesis left off — recounting the sons who went with Jacob to Egypt and the death of Joseph.

- Before Joseph died, what did he confidently declare to his brothers in Genesis 50:24?

The story then jumps ahead about 400 years. The sons of Jacob multiplied and became the people of Israel, a great multitude who filled the land.

- Even with oppression from the greatest superpower in the ancient world, God's purposes and plans for His people continued to prevail. How was Israel's steady growth a confirmation of God's command in Genesis 1:28 and of Jacob's prayer in Genesis 48:15-16?

- Read Exodus 1:15-21. The midwives no doubt feared the king and his punishment if they failed to obey. But their fear of God was greater. How did God reward the brave Egyptian midwives for protecting the children born to the Hebrew women?

As Pharaoh issued a new order to diminish the Hebrew people, God was already setting a rescue plan into motion. Read Exodus 2:1-2. I can't help but wonder if the Levite mother could sense the sacred calling God had already placed on her son's life.

The narrative in Exodus 2:3-10 is one of the most beautiful examples of God's providence in the Old Testament. The river that Pharaoh intended to be a tool of destruction (Exodus 1:22) was used by God as a conduit for deliverance. God also orchestrated His plan using courageous women.

- Write down each female God works through in Chapter 2 and how their bravery played a role in His plan.

Read about Moses' encounters in Exodus 2:11-15. While his intentions were good, he acted in the flesh rather than by God's prompting, and he suffered negative consequences for doing so. Hunted by the evil king, Moses spent 40 years in Midian as a fugitive and voluntary exile.

Sometimes we find ourselves in a proverbial desert because we have brought it upon ourselves. Sometimes, however, God leads us into the desert in preparation for a call to ministry. For Moses, it was both. During his quiet season in Midian, he grew in maturity, humility and servant leadership.

- How has God used a "desert" or waiting period in your life as a catalyst for spiritual growth or ministry training? How does it encourage you to keep pressing on when you feel like you're wasting or losing time?

In his commentary on Exodus, Warren Wiersbe wrote, "Like Joseph's thirteen years as a slave in Egypt and Paul's three years' hiatus after his conversion (Galatians 1:16-17), Moses' 40 years of waiting and working prepared him for a lifetime of faithful ministry. God doesn't lay hands suddenly on His servants but takes time to equip them for their work." [1]

We conclude our study today by looking at the plight of the Israelites from God's point of view. Read Exodus 2:24-25 and fill in the blanks.

- "And God _____ their groaning, and God _____ his covenant with Abraham, with Isaac, and with Jacob. God _____ the people of Israel—and God _____."

The Hebrew word for "knew" can also be translated as "understood" or "being concerned." God was not oblivious or indifferent to their suffering. In fact, their agony moved Him to remember His covenantal promise of salvation. And whenever the Bible speaks of God remembering, action follows. [2]

- James records another instance of God hearing the cries of the oppressed. Read James 5:1-6. What do these verses reveal to you about God's view on oppression?

Friend, whatever hardship you're facing today, God sees you. He hears your cries — even the unspoken pleas emanating from your heart. Never doubt for a moment whether God knows or cares about your struggle.

- According to Psalm 121:5, 8, what is God doing, both now and forevermore? The word "keep" can be translated, "watch over." How does this truth comfort and encourage you?

DAY two

SCRIPTURE READING: Exodus 3:1-12

MAJOR MOMENT: God called Moses to deliver the Israelites out of Egypt.

Throughout the book of Exodus, we will see Moses performing many roles that were ultimately fulfilled by Jesus. In today's study, you will notice several connections and parallels in their lives.

At this point in the story, Moses had left the comforts of a palace and his privileged lifestyle as a prince in order to identify with his people group — the Hebrews. But through his (imperfect) efforts to seek justice and peace, he found himself misunderstood and mocked by his own people. Hunted by the evil king, Moses had no choice but to flee to Midian, where he married, had a son, and settled into a quiet life until the Egyptian ruler's death.

- In Exodus 3:1, what was Moses doing for his father-in-law?

- How does this vocation and Moses' story thus far remind you of Jesus? Write down any similarities you notice. Use the chart on page 15 if you need some help.

Horeb is mentioned in Exodus 3:1 as *"the mountain of God,"* and is believed to be an interchangeable title for the peak that was called Mount Sinai. It was here that God appeared to Moses in the form of fire.

- Read the following verses: Exodus 19:18; Exodus 40:38; Nehemiah 9:19; Numbers 14:14. According to these scriptures, what does the fire symbolize for God's people? What does it reveal about the heart of God?

After an encounter with God speaking from a burning bush, Moses suddenly found himself commissioned with a new role — deliverer. And at the ripe age of 80 years old! In verse 11, Moses asked God how he was qualified to negotiate with Pharaoh and secure Israel's freedom. Instead of listing out Moses' strengths and gifts, God turned the focus to Himself.

- God's response and promise to Moses in Exodus 3:12 was *"I will _____ ..."*

- How does God's presence comfort you when you're feeling ill-equipped for a task He's called you to?

In the Old Testament, mentions of God being "with" someone meant that His power and Spirit enabled them to carry out their divine assignments.

- According to 2 Timothy 3:16-17; Hebrews 13:20-21; and 2 Corinthians 3:5, how does God equip believers today to live out their callings?

Faith is always an element in obedience to God's call. In Exodus 3:12, God promised Moses that he would worship on that same mountain after leading the Israelites out of Egypt, and that this would be a sign that God had sent Him. But given that the sign would occur after the victory, Moses still had a choice of whether to believe God and act in faith. As Bible scholar John N. Oswalt notes in his commentary on Exodus, "Signs do not produce faith. Rather, at a later date they confirm that the faith position taken earlier was the correct one... The fact that God is confident enough of the outcome to make such a prediction helps to encourage faith, but it does not create faith where none exists." [3]

- What does God want you to personally trust Him for today?

DAY *three*

SCRIPTURE READING: Exodus 3:13-15

MAJOR MOMENT: God revealed His name — Yahweh — to Moses.

From the beginning of creation, God intended to be more than a distant, nameless, unapproachable being. In today's reading, God's desire for intimate relationship becomes evident in His conversation with Moses.

Because the Egyptian culture worshipped numerous gods with many different names, Moses likely felt the need to clarify God's identity to the Israelites.

- In Exodus 3:14, what was God's response when Moses asked His name?

While others who lived before Moses knew God's name very early, (See Seth, Genesis 4:26; Noah, Genesis 9:26; Abraham, Genesis 12:8; Isaac, Genesis 26:25; Jacob, Genesis 28:16; Laban, Genesis 30:27) God used Moses' question as an opportunity to remind His people about his personal name, which provided insight into His nature and character. Yahweh (which corresponds to the four Hebrew consonants YHWH) is connected to the Hebrew verb *hayah* that means "to be." It has traditionally been translated as "the LORD" (with small capital letters) or "I AM."

It might seem like God revealed absolutely nothing about Himself... "I AM WHO I AM" sounds like a circular riddle with no answer. But it actually conveys His infinite nature! Bible scholars have elaborated on many different meanings and potential nuances of the name "I AM," but here are some of the most commonly suggested interpretations:

HIS BEING IS **SELF-SUFFICIENT.**
He IS ... regardless of anything that does or doesn't happen.

HIS CHARACTER IS **IMMUTABLE.**
He is the same yesterday, today and tomorrow.

HIS EXISTENCE IS **ETERNAL.**
He has always been, and will eternally be, God.

HE HIMSELF IS **CENTRAL.**
God is at the center of all things.

As Tony Merida suggests in his commentary, in declaring His name I AM, "God tells Moses that the most important thing about his mission is God Himself!" [4] Moses had nothing to fear because God was everything he needed.

- Read Romans 11:36, and fill in the blanks.

    "For _____ him and _____ him and _____ him are _____ _____. To him be glory forever. Amen."

- In light of these explanations of I AM, read Jesus' words in John 8:58 and record your thoughts on what He meant.

- How does John 1:1-4 reinforce Jesus' statement in John 8:58?

Recorded throughout the Gospel of John, Jesus took the "I AM" name one step further to reveal more about His nature and His role as the Savior. Look up the following verses and fill in the blanks.

- John 6:35 *"I am the* _____ *of* _____."
- John 8:12 *"I am the* _____ *of the* _____."
- John 10:7,9 *"I am the* _____ *of the* _____."
- John 10:11,14 *"I am the* _____ _____."
- John 11:25 *"I am the* _____ *and the* _____."
- John 14:6 *"I am the* _____, *the* _____, *and the* _____."
- John 15:1 *"I am the* _____ _____."

Praise God today by filling in the blank with a Name of God or role that resonates most with you at the moment (i.e., Healer, Teacher, Redeemer, Comforter, Heavenly Father). Imagine Him whispering in your ear,

"Beloved, I AM your _____."

HOW DO I GET THROUGH THIS?

DAY *four*

SCRIPTURE READING: Exodus 3:16-22

MAJOR MOMENT: God revealed His plan to bring the Israelites out of slavery in Egypt and into the promised land.

In Exodus 3:16, God commanded Moses to identify Him to the elders of Israel as the God of their fathers — Abraham, Isaac and Jacob. God evidently believed this reference would mean something to His people. Look up the following Bible passages and record God's promises to each patriarch.

PATRIARCH	SCRIPTURE REFERENCE	PROMISE FROM GOD
Abraham	Genesis 12:1-3	
Isaac	Genesis 26:3-4	
Jacob	Genesis 35:9-12	

- In Genesis 15:12-16, God gave Abraham a glimpse of the future. What did He say would happen to Abraham's offspring?

We don't know whether Abraham shared this vision with younger generations, but it's plausible that the promise was passed down orally to each son along with God's covenant to provide innumerable descendants, fruitful land and blessings through Abraham's line. [5]

- How might the Israelites have gained hope by recalling the divine promises to their ancestors?

Read Exodus 3:17-22. Similar to Abraham's experience, Moses was informed by God of how the plan for deliverance would unfold. The prediction included both good news and bad news.

- Why do you think God disclosed these details, particularly Pharaoh's rejection, to Moses?

- What did God's foreknowledge of the events reveal about Himself?

In Exodus 3:18, Moses was instructed to tell Pharaoh that *"the Lord, the God of the Hebrews, has _____ _____ _____."* Again, the theme of God's presence with His people becomes evident.

Moses was also instructed to make a surprising request: permission for the Israelites to take a three-day journey to offer sacrifices and worship. In his commentary on Exodus, John N. Oswalt explains that worship was "not merely a 'smokescreen' to cover the real motive for the request, namely, escape. In fact, it expresses the real reason for the Exodus: that Israel might worship the Lord rightly." [6]

Notice that Moses' request mentioned both God's involvement and the trip's purpose of worship. This should have been clear to Pharaoh that God was at the center of the plea, had he truly been listening.

- Not only did God intend to deliver the Israelites from slavery so they could worship freely, but He also wanted the Egyptians to know what? (See Exodus 7:5.)

The Hebrew word for "the Lord" in Exodus 7:5 is the same name that God revealed to Moses at the burning bush in Exodus 3:13-15. As we learned in our study on Day 3, Yahweh's name reminds us that He is central ... central to all activities, missions, rituals, worship and, most importantly, deliverance.

- Reflect on any areas of your life where you need to make the Lord central.

At the end of Chapter 3, we read that the Israelites would escape Egypt but not leave empty-handed. God's pattern is to go above and beyond our expectations or hopes, and divine favor against the Egyptians would set up the Hebrew people to thrive in their new life of freedom and faith. When God calls, He also equips and provides.

DAY *five*

SCRIPTURE READING: Exodus 4:1-9

MAJOR MOMENT: God gave three miraculous signs to authenticate Moses' testimony and instructions to the Israelites.

God gave His word that the Israelites would believe Moses' message, but the reluctant leader continued to protest.

HIS FIRST QUESTION HAD BEEN
"Who am I?" (Exodus 3:11)

HIS SECOND QUESTION WAS, IN ESSENCE,
"Who are you?" (Exodus 3:13)

Moses then focused his doubts on a third party: the Israelites. (Exodus 4:1)

- Why might Moses have felt so uncertain of the Israelites' reception of him?

Based on Moses' history and life experience, he had some valid reasons to question the success of his calling. But the outcomes of God's missions have never been dependent on human qualifications or efforts.

- Read David's prayer in Psalm 60:11-12, preferably in the NIV translation if available, and fill in the blanks.

    "Give us aid against the enemy, for human help is _____. With _____ we will gain the victory and _____ will trample down our enemies."

- Is there an area of your life where you feel defeated because you're trusting in yourself instead of in God? What can you do differently?

Out of patience and graciousness, God gave Moses three signs to perform before the Israelites to prove he was Yahweh's chosen leader. Read the verses below and record each of the miracles as we explore their significance.

MIRACLE #1: Read Exodus 4:2-5.

_____

Ancient Egyptians considered both a staff and a snake to represent power for priests, magicians or pharaohs. A pharaoh's headdress even featured a cobra to symbolize royalty and divine authority. Through this first miracle, God was perhaps demonstrating His sovereignty in Egyptian territory using their very own symbols of power.

MIRACLE #2: Read Exodus 4:6-7.

_____

Skin ailments were common in ancient Egypt and thought to be a punishment from the various gods and goddesses. [7] By inflicting a disease and then curing it, God demonstrated authority over sickness. Peter Enns says in his commentary, "It may also prefigure Israel's experience: God will take an unclean nation and make it clean." [8]

MIRACLE #3: Read Exodus 4:8-9.

_____

According to Egyptian creation accounts, the Nile river was the original source of life. By changing the water into blood, God was proving dominion over what Egypt saw as the nation's life-giver and sustaining force, and well as over all of nature and its elements. [9]

These three signs were probably as much for Moses' assurance as for the Israelites'. It was also an exercise in obedient faith. In the process of demonstrating His power and control, God urged Moses to act in faith by grabbing the snake by the tail — a risky move that would certainly be foolish outside of the Lord's command. God can accomplish incredible work through every one of us, but He requires our cooperation and trust.

- Celebration of God's faithfulness in the past strengthens our faith for the future. Write a brief prayer of thanksgiving and praise for how God has provided and been present for you during an uncertain time.

WEEKEND REFLECTIONS

We're only a few chapters into Exodus, and the passages have already been rich with reminders of God's promises and provision! True to His covenant, God made a way to preserve and protect the descendants of Abraham, Isaac and Jacob through raising up a deliverer. He also faithfully equipped Moses for the mission with His presence, people to help (the elders) and power to prove His authority.

With so many dramatic events and details, we don't want to miss a crucial part of God's promise to Moses that's recorded in Exodus 3:17. God wanted to rescue His people out of slavery so He could bring them into a land of hope and blessing ... a fertile land *"flowing with milk and honey."* God has such a place awaiting us too ... a new heaven and a new earth where all things will be made new and we will live in perfect and unhindered relationship with God. (Revelation 21:1-5)

PRAYER

Father, Your plans and Your purposes far exceed anything we could think up ourselves. Thank You for preserving both Your people and the writings of Moses so we can trace Your gracious and saving hand throughout history! Lord, turn any unbelief in our hearts to confidence in You. Remind us of how You have faithfully delivered us and provided for us in the past. Let us not take for granted the gift and privilege of Your constant presence!

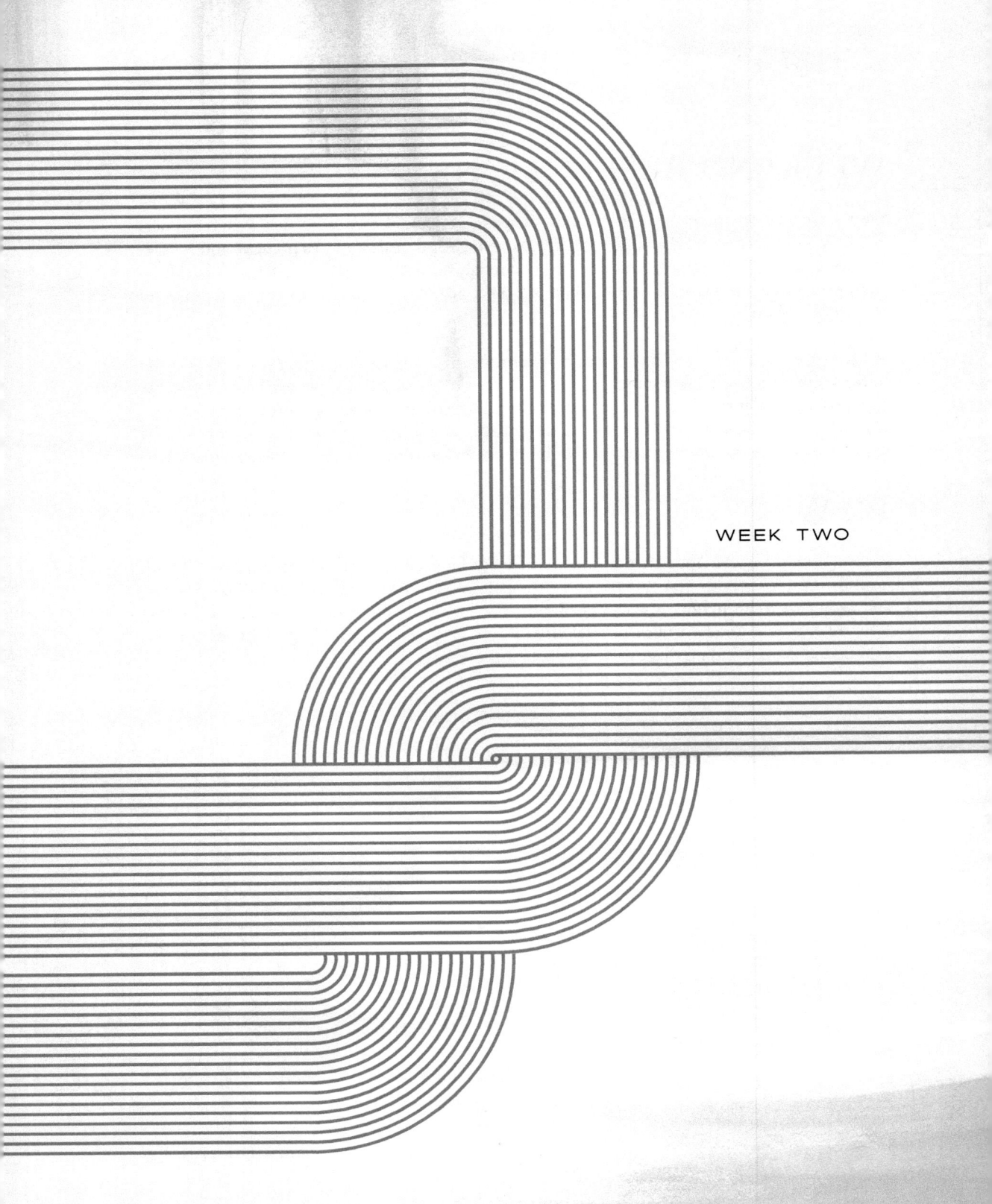

DAY SIX

SCRIPTURE READING: Exodus 4:10-18
MAJOR MOMENT: Moses protested but was assured by God.

Today's reading continues Moses' questioning of God's call on his life, this time due to his speech and verbal communication. There's no way to know exactly why Moses voiced concern about his speech. Scholars speculate it could have been because of how long he had been away from Egypt, so he felt unrehearsed in their language, or possibly because he spent so much time tending sheep that he had lost eloquence. [1]

It's reasonable to think the people would have expected an eloquent, well-spoken leader to rescue them and address Pharaoh on their behalf. However, God did not tell Moses he would make him eloquent; instead, God appealed to Moses to trust Him to provide. He gave Moses both a promise and provision.

According to Exodus 4:12,
- What was the promise?

- What was the provision?

God *promised* Moses that He would help him speak and that He would provide the words by teaching Moses what to speak. While Moses focused on himself, God reminded Moses "I AM" was with his mouth. [2]

When Jesus sent out the 12 disciples, He gave them similar encouragement:

"When they deliver you over, do not be anxious how you are to speak or what you are to say, for what you are to say will be given to you in that hour. For it is not you who speak, but the Spirit of your Father speaking through you" (Matthew 10:19-20).

According to Matthew 10:19-20,
- When did Jesus say His disciples would be given what to say?

- Who did Jesus say would speak?

Just as God pointed Moses to His promise and provision, Jesus assures us, as His disciples, that He will be with us and work through us when we follow Him.

- Has God called you to do something you don't feel equipped to do?

- How might shifting your perspective from yourself and your ability to God and His faithfulness help move you forward?

DAY seven

SCRIPTURE READING: Exodus 4:19-31

MAJOR MOMENT: Moses returned to Egypt.

Today's reading introduces us to the first mention in Scripture of God calling Israel His son, but not just any son:

"Then you shall say to Pharaoh, 'Thus says the Lord, Israel is my _____ son.'"
Exodus 4:22

To fully grasp the significance of God's designation of Israel as His firstborn son, it's important to know what that implied to the original hearer of these words. Being the firstborn son came with rights, privileges and responsibilities. [3]

In the ancient world, the firstborn son would have been favored with inheritance and represented the father in many ways as he grew in age. Additionally, in ancient Israel, the firstborn son would have traditionally been devoted to God. [4] By calling Israel His firstborn son, God revealed the heart of a special, loving relationship to His people. [5]

Our own earthly experiences of a father-and-child relationship can sometimes make it difficult to grasp the blessing connected with this intimate relationship between God and His people.

- How has an earthly experience influenced your view of God as Father?

- How does understanding sonship as a personal, loving relationship with God change your perspective?

"He [Jesus] is the image of the invisible God, the firstborn of all creation" (Colossians 1:15).

- According to Colossians 1:15, who is the firstborn?

Just as God revealed Israel to be His firstborn son, we now understand Jesus is God's sinless Son and ultimate redemption for His people. (Matthew 3:17) Because of Christ, we, too, can be children of God. (1 John 3:1)

"The Spirit himself bears witness with our spirit that we are children of God, and if children, then heirs—heirs of God and fellow heirs with Christ, provided we suffer with him in order that we may also be glorified with him" (Romans 8:16-17).

- The position of being God's child gives us the privilege to become what?

- Our privilege as God's children and heirs does not come without responsibility. We are fellow heirs with Christ provided we what?

- How can understanding the privileges and responsibilities of being a child of God encourage you when you face circumstances that make you feel like you want to give up?

DAY *eight*

SCRIPTURE READING: Exodus 5:1-14

MAJOR MOMENT: Moses told Pharaoh to let the people go.

Today's passage records the first time Pharaoh refused to let God's people go; however, it wouldn't be the last time.

The Egyptian Pharaoh would have been a devotee of, representative of, and human focal point for Egypt's gods. [6] To acknowledge and obey the Lord would have diminished his authority and control; therefore, he dismissed Moses and Aaron's request as if it was nonsense.

- According to Exodus 5:2, what was Pharaoh's reason for refusing to let Israel go?

The Hebrew word translated "know" in Exodus 5:2 is *yada'*. [7] In the six chapters that follow Exodus 5, this Hebrew word is repeated multiple times. From this point forward, God will act in order that Pharaoh, the Egyptians and Israel might know Him.

- According to Exodus 5:4-5, instead of knowing God, what was Pharaoh concerned about?

Compare Exodus 5:1 to Exodus 5:10-11.

- Who did Moses and Aaron speak for and lead the people to serve?

- Who did the taskmasters speak for and tell the people to serve?

- Based on Exodus 5:6-14, when God's plan to rescue Israel began to unfold, did it get better or worse for Israel?

God's presence does not guarantee immediate results of rescue. Israel needed only to look to her past to see this principle. Both for Abraham and Joseph, God's plan and presence produced challenges and struggles before it culminated in God's promise. [8] Jesus' life showed us this, too.

"He was in the world, and the world was made through him, yet the world did not know him" (John 1:10).

- Describe a time when you found yourself in the midst of challenges or struggles as you followed God.

- How does this part of Israel's story of deliverance help you press on and trust God's faithfulness and plan?

DAY *nine*

SCRIPTURE READING: Exodus 5:15-21

MAJOR MOMENT: The people complained that Moses made things worse.

In Exodus 5:17, Pharaoh repeated the same word he used in verse 8 to describe his analysis of Israel's request. Record that word here:

Depending on what translation you read, it could say *lazy, idle* or even *slackers*. Based on verse 5, D.K. Stuart noted that, "most or all Israelites may at that moment not only have stopped work but amassed somewhere to await the report from the encounter at the palace and perhaps to pray for the immediate success of that encounter." [9]

- Put yourself in Israel's shoes for a moment. If in fact they had been gathered somewhere waiting on good news and ready to leave, how would this sudden change in circumstances have made them feel?

Pharaoh's new demand required the people to scour the land for leftover bits of straw, likely stubble. [10] There would have been no way they could have continued their normal production. The weight of this mandate would have left them drained, desperate and disheartened.

- According to Exodus 5:20-21, where did the opposition to Moses and Aaron come from now?

- Go back and read Exodus 4:31. How did the change in circumstances in Exodus 5 alter Israel's attitude?

HOW DO I GET THROUGH THIS?

Despite being warned that Pharaoh's heart would be hardened toward their request, scholars believe the extent of Pharaoh's resistance — and the consequences that came with it — likely caught Moses, Aaron and the people off guard. [11] Pharaoh's tactics caused the Israelites to turn against the very ones sent by God to deliver them from Egypt.

- Can you think of a time when your circumstances didn't unfold the way you expected them to?

- How did you respond?

- Is there anything you would have done differently?

DAY ten

SCRIPTURE READING: Exodus 5:22-6:12
MAJOR MOMENT: Moses complained to God.

In Exodus 5:22, Moses posed two questions to God. Both begin with the word *"why."*

- Why _____?

- Why _____?

One scholar identified Moses' attitude as an "I told you so" approach and added that the literal translation of Moses' question reads, *"Why did you ever send me [in the first place]?"* [12]

The next nine verses record God's answer to Moses' protest. Four times in Exodus 6:1-9, God says, *"I am the Lord"* (vv. 1, 6, 7, 9). Exodus 6:2 records two names of God.

- According to Exodus 6:2, by what name did God say He revealed Himself to Abraham, Issac and Jacob? What name did He not reveal to them?

- By what name did He say He would fully make Himself known to Israel? (v. 6)

The patriarchs knew God by the name *El Shaddai* or God Almighty. With the statement that He would now fully reveal the character of His name *Yahweh*, God assured Moses He was the same God the patriarchs worshipped and that He would fulfill the promises He made to them. [13] Exodus 6:6-8 records seven "I will" statements by God. Fill in the blanks below with what God said He would do:

"'I WILL _____ FROM UNDER THE BURDENS OF THE EGYPTIANS. AND I WILL _____ FROM SLAVERY TO THEM. AND I WILL _____ WITH AN OUTSTRETCHED ARM AND WITH GREAT ACTS OF JUDGMENT. I WILL _____. AND I WILL _____, AND YOU SHALL KNOW THAT I AM THE LORD YOUR GOD, WHO HAS BROUGHT YOU OUT FROM UNDER THE BURDENS OF THE EGYPTIANS. I WILL _____ THAT I SWORE TO GIVE TO ABRAHAM, TO ISAAC, AND TO JACOB. I WILL _____ FOR A POSSESSION. I AM THE LORD.'"

HOW DO I GET THROUGH THIS?

- How did Israel respond to God's promises? (v. 9a)

- Why didn't they listen? (v. 9b)

The Hebrew word translated "broken spirit" in verse 9 is *qotser*. It is defined as "shortness of spirit," meaning both anguish and impatience. [14]

- Have you ever grown impatient with God's plan and promises?

- How does reflecting on God's promises help you trust His timing?

WEEKEND REFLECTIONS

We may not always feel capable to follow God's calling. Sometimes God will call us to do things we feel ill-equipped for. Sometimes our circumstances may tempt us to give up or doubt His promises, but God's calling is not about us and our ability; it's about Him. As God's faithfulness to Moses and Israel shows us, His promises are not compromised by resistance, and His calling is not cancelled because of circumstances.

PRAYER

Dear God, I'm amazed at how the circumstances of Your people so many years ago feel so familiar to me today. Thank You for reminding me that earthly challenges don't change Your eternal, perfect plan. When I'm faced with circumstances that make me give up, help me trust Your timing and press on with my eyes fixed on You. In Jesus' name, amen.

WEEK THREE

DAY *eleven*

SCRIPTURE READING: Exodus 6:13-27

MAJOR MOMENT: The genealogy of Moses and Aaron were recorded.

Last week's study finished with Moses questioning God's plan and his place in that plan. The first verse of today's reading gives a firm answer.

"But the Lord spoke to Moses and Aaron and gave them a charge about the people of Israel and about Pharaoh king of Egypt: to bring the people of Israel out of the land of Egypt" (Exodus 6:13).

- Who did God give Moses a charge about? (There are two answers.)

- What was that charge?

- Did Moses' concerns or the current circumstances change God's command or His plan?

Exodus 6:14-25 records a genealogical list. This genealogical list is placed here in the exodus story for several reasons, one of which is to trace the lineage of Aaron and Moses. [1] Let's break it down so we can better understand it.

- Which three sons of Israel are listed with their descendants? (vv. 14-16)

- From here, the genealogy focuses on the tribe of Levi. What are the names of Levi's three sons? (v. 16)

- After recording the sons of Levi's firstborn, the sons of his son Kohath are listed. Write those here:

- Who was Amram? (v. 20)

Exodus 6:23-25 records all the way through Aaron's grandson, Phinehas. While we haven't encountered the names on this section of the list yet, as the plot of the exodus develops, we will see reasons why Moses may have chosen to include these names.

This section closes with the repetition of the names, Moses and Aaron, (vv. 26-27) so that it "unmistakably links the two brothers with both the genealogy [of Israel] and the exodus." [2]

The placement of this genealogy comes at a turning point in the story of God's deliverance of His people from slavery in Egypt.

- Why would it be important for the reader to have no doubt about who Moses and Aaron are?

DAY *twelve*

SCRIPTURE READING: Exodus 6:28-7:13

MAJOR MOMENT: Moses and Aaron performed the first sign before Pharaoh.

Today's reading sets the stage for the sparring between the Lord and Pharaoh. At first glance, it may appear that Pharaoh's magicians did the same thing as Moses and Aaron, but a closer look at Exodus 7:10-11 reveals some key differences.

"So Moses and Aaron went to Pharaoh and did just as the Lord commanded. Aaron cast down his staff before Pharaoh and his servants, and it became a serpent" (Exodus 7:10).

"Then Pharaoh summoned the wise men and the sorcerers, and they, the magicians of Egypt, also did the same by their secret arts" (Exodus 7:11).

- According to Exodus 7:10, Moses and Aaron went to Pharaoh and did _____ _____.

- According to Exodus 7:11, Pharaoh _____ the wise men and sorcerers and they did the same by their _____.

- How does God's power differ from Pharaoh's "power"?

The word translated "secret arts" can also be translated "trickery." [3] Moses and Aaron didn't *summon* power or employ *trickery* when Aaron's staff became a serpent; instead, they simply obeyed God's command.

The result of this initial encounter foretells the final result of Pharaoh's battle with God. The word used to describe how Aaron's snake *swallowed* the other staffs is used only twice in Scripture: here in Exodus 7:12, and again in Exodus 15 to describe how the Red Sea *swallowed* the Egyptian army when it pursued the rescued Israel. [4]

This first demonstration of God's sovereignty and power, and Pharaoh's resistance, sets in motion the 10 plagues that follow. John Calvin observes,

"It was, indeed, possible for God to overwhelm him [Pharaoh] at once, by a single nod, so that he should even fall down dead at the very sight of Moses; but ... He wished to shew that, against all the strivings and devices of Satan, against the madness of the ungodly, and all worldly hindrances, His hand must always prevail; and to leave us no room to doubt, but that whatever we see opposing us will at length be overcome by him." [5]

- How does this first example of God's prevailing power encourage you in your circumstances today?

DAY *thirteen*

SCRIPTURE READING: Exodus 7:14-8:32
MAJOR MOMENT: God sent plagues of blood, frogs, gnats and flies.

The first two plagues involved the Nile River and would have immediately gotten the attention of every Egyptian for a couple of reasons. First, Egypt's civilization depended on the waters of the Nile. Second, the Nile River was worshipped as a god in Egypt. Therefore, this attack on the Nile was an attack on the security and prosperity of the country as well as an attack on Egypt's gods. [6]

The first plague turned the water in the Nile to blood.
- How does Exodus 7:21 describe the Nile River?

- Exodus 7:23 tells us Pharaoh did not take this to heart. Where did he go?

The second plague brought frogs up out of the Nile.
- Where does Exodus 8:3 say the frogs will go?

- How does Exodus 8:14 describe the land?

Without the retreat of his house, and with the land now stinking like the Nile, Pharaoh pleaded with Moses to ask God to take away the frogs and promised to let the people go. However, his change of heart didn't last long. (Exodus 8:15)

The third plague of gnats may seem out of place since it doesn't follow the same pattern as the other plagues; however, it fits nicely into the pattern of the plagues as a whole. The first nine plagues come in a series of three, with the last plague in every series including no forewarning, time of warning, or instruction formula. [7]

- According to Exodus 8:18, what happened with the magicians after God turned the dust to gnats?

- After the fourth plague of flies, how does Exodus 8:24 describe the land?

The land went from stinky to ruined, and after the second plague, Pharaoh's magicians were no longer able to produce God's wonders. Yet, instead of obeying God, Pharaoh tried to bargain with Him.

- Have you ever tried to bargain with God?

- What was the result of your conditional obedience?

HOW DO I GET THROUGH THIS?

DAY *fourteen*

SCRIPTURE READING: Exodus 9:1-10:20

MAJOR MOMENT: God sent plagues of disease, boils, hail and locusts.

Exodus 9:3 records two things about the fifth plague that we have not read before this point.

"Behold, the hand of the Lord will fall with a very severe plague upon your livestock that are in the field, the horses, the donkeys, the camels, the herds, and the flocks" (Exodus 9:3).

According to this verse,

- What would fall?

- What kind of plague would this be?

Before now, only the finger of God had been mentioned in the plagues. (Exodus 8:19) This plague, however, would bring the full force of God's hand against Pharaoh and the Egyptians, as it was the first plague that brought with it death.

Exodus 9:14-16 summarizes the purpose of the entire exodus story. Verses 14 and 16 both end with a phrase that begins with the words *"so that."* Record those phrases here:

- So that _____.

- So that _____.

The sixth plague presents a point of intensification in the story. Douglas Stewart noted, "The prior plagues, troublesome as they were, were essentially preliminary and that now a series of developments that would really do damage to Egypt—including actually taking of human life." [8]

Exodus 9:20-21 details the actions of two different responses to God.

- What were the two responses?

- According to Exodus 9:17 and 10:3, what was the root of why Pharaoh and some of his servants did not pay attention to the word of the Lord?

The plague of locusts brought out another purpose for God's signs of divine power.

- According to Exodus 10:2, what did God reveal about the purpose of the plagues?

Peter Enns says, "God's actions in Egypt with the Exodus generation are not meant to be kept secret. They must be told and remembered in future generations." [9]

- How can God's presence, power and faithfulness in your times of trial become a catalyst for you to make Him known to the next generation?

DAY *fifteen*

SCRIPTURE READING: Exodus 10:21-29
MAJOR MOMENT: God sent a plague of darkness.

The ninth plague brought darkness over the land of Egypt.

- According to Exodus 10:23, what two things happened as a result of this darkness?

We also learned that the darkness blanketed Egypt for three days.

- Have you ever been without electricity?

- Describe some things that would happen and how you would feel if you went three days without power.

In modern times, we are accustomed to having manufactured light, so to fully grasp the weight of this plague, it will be helpful to see it through the eyes of ancient Egypt.

Douglas Stewart describes their condition: "They closed up their cities at night, barred their courtyard gates, and locked their house doors. People abroad in the nighttime were assumed to be criminals and, typically, in fact were." [10]

In the story of creation, darkness was the first thing God addressed.

"The earth was without form and void, and darkness was over the face of the deep ... And God said, 'Let there be light,' and there was light" (Genesis 1:2-3).

Throughout Scripture, darkness represents chaos and death. God opened creation by addressing the physical darkness, but God did not only provide an answer to physical darkness. [11]

"Jesus spoke to them, saying, 'I am the light of the world. Whoever follows me will not walk in darkness, but will have the light of life'" (John 8:12).

- Describe a time when you have walked in physical darkness. Did you run into anything? Did you choose not to move at all?

- Now think of a time in your life when you walked in spiritual darkness. What are some differences between walking in spiritual darkness and having the light of life?

"When we receive Jesus, the Light of the World, as our Lord and Savior, He allows us to become light to the world" (Matthew 5:14-16).

- How does experiencing the light of Christ motivate you to share His light with the world?

- What is one practical way you will do that today?

WEEKEND REFLECTIONS

The story of the plagues puts God's power on display. As we close this week of study, pause to give these great acts of God their due wonder. Let this account of God's complete control over His creation lead you to exalt Him to His proper place of Almighty and All-Powerful and worship Him as Yahweh.

PRAYER

Dear God, as I consider the extent of Your glory, beauty and power revealed to me each day through Your creation, I'm ashamed at how often I overlook it. I bow my head and lift my hands today to You, Almighty God. The next time I worry about how I will get through, draw my heart to this display of Your power. In Jesus' name, amen.

THE
PLAGUES

When the Lord brought the 10 plagues on Pharaoh and the Egyptians, He demonstrated His power over nature, disease and death. He also specifically showed His sovereignty over the false gods of the Egyptians. In Exodus 12:12, God said: *"For I will pass through the land of Egypt that night, and I will strike all the firstborn in the land of Egypt, both man and beast;* **and on all the gods of Egypt I will execute judgments: I am the LORD***"* (emphasis added). In the chart below, you can see the connections between each of the plagues and one or more of the revered Egyptian gods.

PLAGUE	EGYPTIAN GODS
1. NILE TURNED TO BLOOD	The Egyptians worshipped the river gods Osiris, Nu and Hapi. Hapi was considered the "giver of life."
2. FROGS	The goddess of childbirth, Heqet, was often portrayed with the head of a frog. The Egyptians believed she controlled the frog population and assisted women in childbirth.
3. GNATS	The Egyptians believed that Pharaoh had the divine ability to maintain order in creation, which they referred to as *ma'at*. When gnats covered all people and animals, this power of Pharaoh's was proved worthless.

4. FLIES	There are a few possibilities for the target of this plague: Beelzebub, who protected them against swarms of insects and natural disasters; Kheprer, the god of resurrection, who was often depicted as a beetle; and Uatchit, who was believed to manifest himself as an egg-laying fly.
5. DEATH OF EGYPTIAN LIVESTOCK	Many of the Egyptian gods were portrayed as cattle or bulls. These included Isis, the queen of the gods, and Hathor, a goddess who protected Pharaoh. Some Egyptians worshipped bulls and viewed them as a symbol of fertility.
6. BOILS	The Egyptians looked to many gods and goddesses for protection from disease or for physical healing, including Amon, Thoth, Imhotep and Sekhmet.
7. HAIL	Many Egyptian gods and goddesses were connected with the weather and sky. Seth came in the wind and storms, Shu held up the atmosphere, and Nut was the sky goddess.
8. LOCUSTS DESTROY THE CROPS	Egyptians also trusted their gods and goddesses to supply them with food. Min was the god of crops, while Anubis guarded the fields and Senehem gave protection from pests.
9. DARKNESS	The Egyptians worshipped the sun and viewed the sun god, Amon-Re, to be their creator and the most powerful of all their gods.
10. DEATH OF EGYPTIAN FIRSTBORN	The Egyptians believed death was ruled by Osiris, the god of the dead, and his assistant Anubis, god of the underworld. Also, Pharaoh was considered a son of the sun god, Amon-Re. Therefore, the death of his son (the successor to his god-like throne) is significant.

WEEK FOUR

DAY sixteen

SCRIPTURE READING: Exodus 11:1– 12:28

MAJOR MOMENT: The final plague is revealed, and God gave instructions for the Passover.

In Exodus 11, God pronounced the 10th and final plague upon Egypt: the death of every firstborn.

- Exodus 11:5: God spoke through Moses that "_____ *firstborn in the land of Egypt shall die, from the firstborn of* _____..., *even to the firstborn of the* _____... *and all the firstborn of the* _____."

- Why did Pharaoh refuse to heed this last plague? (Exodus 11:9-10)

Beginning in Chapter 12, specific instructions for every aspect of the Passover were detailed by God. This was not an idea of any mere human; it was straight from the throne room of heaven — *"It is the LORD'S Passover"* (Exodus 12:11). A one-year-old male lamb (without blemish) was to be killed in a certain way, roasted in a certain way and eaten in a certain way along with bitter herbs and unleavened bread. The lamb's blood was to be put on the doorposts of their homes. Note the foreshadowing of a similar redemption which would eventually come through Jesus Christ.

The Passover lamb foreshadowed **Jesus,** our "_____" (1 Corinthians 5:7).

The redemption of Israel through the blood of the unblemished lamb was to foreshadow **Jesus,** who would redeem us "... *with the precious blood of Christ, like that of a lamb without* _____ *or* _____" (1 Peter 1:19).

The blood of the lamb freed God's people from the bondage of Egypt, just as Jesus *"freed us from our sins* _____" (Revelation 1:5).

According to John 13:1, Jesus was crucified during the week of _____.

HOW DO I GET THROUGH THIS?

D.A. Carson explains, "death doesn't pass over them *(Israel)* on the ground of the intensity or the clarity of the faith exercised, but on the ground of the blood of the lamb. That's what silences the accuser." [1] Jesus, the Lamb of God, silenced the accuser once and for all, freeing us from the slavery of sin and the penalty of death through the cross. This final act of God's substitutionary atonement gives us hope to press on because sin can no longer enslave us.

The Lord also commanded the observance of the Feast of Unleavened Bread beginning the day after the observance of Passover.

- What did God want His children to remember by celebrating the Feast of Unleavened Bread? (Exodus 12:17)

- Note that in the New Testament, leaven was a symbol of hypocrisy and sin. [2] Rewrite Paul's words in 1 Corinthians 5:8 and Galatians 5:9 using the concept of leaven as sin.

As Jesus celebrated Passover with His disciples, He instructed them in a new observance, a way to remember Him through the bread and the cup representing His body and blood.

- How does our celebration of the Lord's Supper today mirror the Passover meal?

- Write a short prayer of thanksgiving to God for His miracle of salvation in your own life.

DAY seventeen

SCRIPTURE READING: Exodus 12:29-13:16

MAJOR MOMENT: The death of Egypt's firstborn and the consecration of Israel's firstborn were recorded.

In Exodus 12:27-28, after Moses gave the Israelites all the words of God concerning the Passover, *"the people bowed their heads and _____ ... as the LORD had commanded Moses and Aaron, so they did."*

- What do the verses above tell you about the hearts of the Israelites during this time?

The 10th plague of Egypt targeted Pharaoh (who was considered the all-powerful god of Egypt). At midnight, every word that the Lord had proclaimed came to pass. God's judgment was accomplished. *"... there was not a house where someone was not dead"* (Exodus 12:30). Even Pharaoh's firstborn was dead, and all of Egypt knew that Israel's God was GOD.

It was not because the Israelites deserved God's favor that the Lord passed over their houses that night; it was only due to the sacrifice which signified that a substitutionary death had already taken place in that home, the death of a lamb.

In Exodus 13, we read about the consecration of Israel's firstborn. According to Hebrew culture, firstborn sons had special significance; they insured the family's generational security.

- In Exodus 13:2, God told Israel to "_____ to Me _____ _____ firstborn ... both of man and of beast." The word "consecrate" means: "to set apart from the sinful and secular for a special divine use." [3]

HOW DO I GET THROUGH THIS?

As God claimed the firstborn of Israel, He claimed the nation for Himself. God had spared Israel's firstborn for a purpose: His purpose. All that God did was pointing to the fulfillment of a greater firstborn, His Son, who would be sacrificed for the redemption of all humankind.

- *"He (Jesus) is the image of the invisible God, the _____ of all creation"* (Colossians 1:15).

Once the Israelites were out of Egypt, the Lord also remembered them to keep the Passover with the unleavened bread, lamb and bitter herbs as a remembrance. When children in future generations asked about the meaning of this observance, the parents would be able to tell them: " ... *'It is because of what the LORD did for me when I came out of Egypt'"* (Exodus 13:8).

- Why was God concerned about the parents telling their children the meaning of the Passover?

- Why is it important for us to teach the children in our families about the Lord and all He has done for us? (Deuteronomy 6:7)

Charles Spurgeon said it this way: "Let us, brethren, go back to the day in our experience, when we abode in the land of Egypt, working in the brick-kilns of sin, toiling to make ourselves better, and finding it to be of no avail; let us recall that memorable night, the beginning of months, the commencement of a new life in our spirit, and the beginning of an altogether new era in our soul." [4]

DAY eighteen

SCRIPTURE READING: Exodus 13:17-14:31

MAJOR MOMENT: The Israelites crossed the Red Sea.

It is estimated that at least two million people left Egypt after the Passover. God had performed a miraculous work to free His children from the bondage of slavery; however, He was not finished with His miraculous works on behalf of His new nation of Israel.

Exodus 13:17-22 details the beginning of their journey out of Egypt toward the promised land; it was also the beginning of a new nation, a new year and a new life for the people of God. There are three references to God (the LORD) leading them in those six verses. This is important because the path which God chose for them was not the most direct route to Canaan (the land God had promised to their ancestors).

- Why did God **not** lead them by the shortest route? (Exodus 13:17)

- How did the Israelites know that God was leading them? (Exodus 13:20-22)

At the beginning of Chapter 14, the Lord spoke to Moses, giving him insight into the path He had chosen for them. Pharaoh was questioning his decision to free the slaves: *"What is this we have done, that we have let Israel go from serving us?"* (Exodus 14:5). Never underestimate the power of God, for God can and will be glorified, even by the actions of evil men.

- Why did Pharaoh decide to pursue the Israelites? (Exodus 14:8)

- What was God's plan for Pharaoh's army? (Exodus 14:4)

Finding themselves trapped between the Red Sea and the army of Egypt, the Israelites were helpless, hopeless, afraid. In fear, they cried out to God; in anger, they blamed Moses. How quickly they forgot God's power and deliverance just a few days before. Moses, however, believed God's promise to deliver them through the sea, and he lifted his staff over the Red Sea in faith.

- Moses said to the people, "_____, _____, and see the _____ *of the Lord, which he will work for you today. For the Egyptians whom you see today, you shall never see again. The Lord will* _____ *and you have only to be silent"* (Exodus 14:13-14).

- How can you apply Exodus 14:13-14 to circumstances in your life when you want to give up or blame someone else?

As Moses obeyed God, the angel of God (that had **guided** His people, v. 19) moved in between the Israelites and the Egyptians (and **guarded** His people). This "pillar of cloud" also provided light to the Israelites and darkness to the Egyptians. Once the Israelites stepped out in faith, they walked through the sea on dry land and then watched the Egyptian soldiers vanish as the waters were unleashed by the hand of God.

- What were the Egyptians' last words according to Exodus 14:25?

- Take a minute to reflect on God's power: to part the sea; to dry the ground; to hold the waters back until all His people had safely crossed; to confuse Pharaoh's army; to cause the chariots to swerve; to return the waters just in time to destroy all of Pharaoh's army. How does this expand your understanding of Exodus 14:14?

THE EXODUS
FROM EGYPT

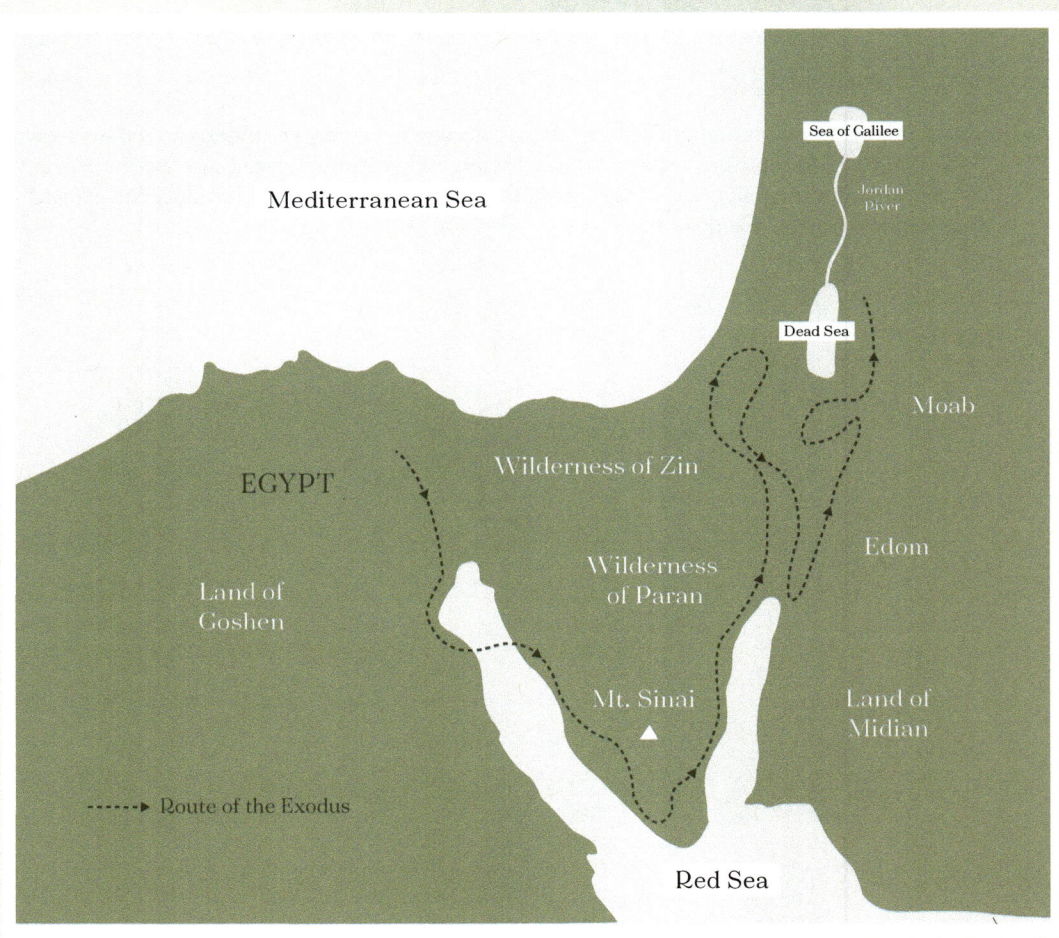

DAY nineteen

SCRIPTURE READING: Exodus 15:1-27

MAJOR MOMENT: Moses and the people sang a song, and bitter water was made sweet.

The fear of the Egyptians was gone; the Israelites had witnessed the mighty power of God as He fought for them and brought them safely to the other side of the sea. With hearts full of praise and thanksgiving, they sang "The Song of Moses." Imagine millions of voices joyfully lifting up their praises to God.

- According to the following verses, list the actions and attributes of God:

    Verse 2: *"The Lord is my _____ and my _____,*

    and he has become my _____;"

    Verse 7: *"In the greatness of your _____ you overthrow your adversaries;*

    you send out your _____; it _____ them like stubble."

    Verse 11: *"Who is like you, O Lord, among the gods?*

    Who is like you, _____ in holiness,

    _____ in glorious deeds, doing wonders?"

    Verse 13: *"You have led in your _____ _____ the people*

    whom you have redeemed; you have guided them by your _____ to your

    holy abode."

- Do any of these verses speak to your heart as you have watched God work in your life?

Moses' song of salvation in Exodus 15:1-18 is our song because the story of the Israelites is our story.

The Israelites were in bondage in Egypt. We were in bondage to sin. (John 8:34)

In God's great mercy, He redeemed the Israelites by the blood of the lamb, and He led them out of bondage into the promised land. In God's great mercy, He redeemed us by the blood of Christ, and He has led us out of bondage of sin and into eternal life.

- Read Ephesian 2:13, and relate this verse to the redemption of the Israelites in Egypt.

How quickly God's people forgot His provision and began to grumble. The desert was hot, water was scarce, and the water they found was bitter. The waters of Marah could not satisfy their thirst, and they began to long for the plentiful, fresh water from the cisterns of Egypt. *"What shall we drink?"* they grumbled to Moses (Exodus 15:24).

Charles Spurgeon said, "What a question! They were at the Red Sea, and God cleft the intervening gulf in twain, through the depths thereof they marched dryshod; there is Marah's water—shall it be more difficult for God to purify than to divide?... Is anything too hard for the Lord?" [5]

Notice that Moses didn't answer the people; he just prayed ... and obeyed.

- According to verse 25, what did God do for His people through Moses?

- Contrast Elim (v. 27) with Marah (vv. 23-25). What conclusions can you draw from the number (12) of springs of fresh water?

- Read John 7:37. How does God's provision at Elim foreshadow God's provision for us through Jesus?

Our journey in this life is much like that of Israel's. Our trials will be many on the journey to the promised land, and there will be times when we want to turn back. However, as we persevere and trust the Lord, He will be with us and will guide us safely home. Jesus tells us, *"In the world you will have tribulation. But take heart; I have overcome the world"* (John 16:33).

DAY twenty

SCRIPTURE READING: Exodus 16:1-17:7

MAJOR MOMENT: Despite the Israelites' grumbling, God sent bread from heaven and water from the rock.

As we follow the wilderness journey of the Israelites, a repetitive cycle comes into focus: the grumbling of the people and the mercy of God. Their grumbling was an outward expression of their inner dissatisfaction — not just toward their circumstances, but toward God. It was evidence of their lack of faith.

- Compare Exodus 16:2 with Exodus 16:8. Who were the people grumbling against?

- How is Israel's lack of faith evidenced according to Exodus 16:3?

- What were the miracles they had experienced just before each of these complaints?

    Exodus 15:22-27 —

    Exodus 16:13-17 —

One month after they left Egypt, the food supply was exhausted, the Israelites forgot God's power, provision and protection and they longed for their former life of slavery in Egypt. In his commentary on this passage, John Wesley said, "Discontent magnifies what is past and vilifies what is present without regards to truth or reason." [6]

God, in His great mercy, showed His loving care and provision three times in Chapter 16:
1. He gave them more of Himself by showing them MORE of His glory. (Exodus 16:9-10)
2. He provided quail (meat) in the evening for them to gather. (Exodus 16:13)
3. He provided manna in the morning for them to gather. (Exodus 16:14)

- What were God's specific instructions regarding the manna? (Exodus 16:16-23)

- What did manna taste like? (Exodus 16:31)

- Just as manna was the bread that sustained life in the wilderness, Jesus says, *"I am the _____ _____ _____; whoever comes to me shall not hunger ... "* (John 6:35).

Even as the supply of manna was always enough for each day and was never exhausted, God's supply for us through His Word is always enough and abundant.

- According to Lamentations 3:22-23, what do the mercies of God and the manna from God have in common?

- In what circumstances of your life do you need to see God's mercies and provision today?

Chapter 17 opens with more grumbling over lack of water. Notice the stark difference between the faithlessness of the people and the faith of Moses. Each time the people complained to him, Moses prayed; each time Moses prayed, God faithfully answered. As Moses obeyed, the Lord provided every need.

- How were God's instructions to Moses in Exodus 17:5-6 a sign of His faithfulness to His children?

John Wesley also wrote about God's amazing grace evidenced through this miracle: "O the wonderful patience and forbearance of God towards provoking sinners! He maintains those that are at war with him and reaches out the hand of his bounty to those that lift up the heel against him." [7]

God's people were thirsty in the wilderness just as we are thirsty today. Jesus is the source of living water; He is the only source that will satisfy our thirsty souls.

- Select one or more of the following verses, allowing Jesus to speak His living water over your soul today. (John 4:14; John 7:37-38; Revelation 22:17). Rewrite the verse in your own words.

- Ask God to reveal and cleanse any "grumbling" in your heart today. (1 John 1:9)

WEEKEND REFLECTIONS

Over the past week, we have walked with Moses and the children of Israel through some of the most powerful events in their history. We've watched the great I AM miraculously move on their behalf to free them from years of slavery in Egypt through the blood of the Passover lamb. We've felt their fear at the Red Sea, trapped between the waters and Pharaoh's army, and we've watched the mighty breath of God blow back the sea and dry the ground, delivering them once and for all from Pharaoh.

Once the fear of Egypt was behind them, new fears arose at every turn: where could they find fresh water in the desert and what about food for two million people? Yet every time there was a need, God abundantly provided. His mercy and grace were tangibly displayed, even in the midst of their grumbling and complaining.

Traveling with Israel in their journey through the desert wilderness, I am reminded that in every story of Israel's miracles, we see Jesus, God's provision for us. Jesus is our Passover Lamb that was slain as our substitutionary sacrifice; Jesus is the rock in the wilderness that was struck in order to provide the rivers of living water through His Spirit in us; Jesus is the manna from heaven, our Bread of Life that feeds our hungry souls with fresh nourishment from His Word. Jesus was the embodiment of God's mercy and grace, and we find in Him the abundant answer to our every need. The same God who was for Israel and with Israel is for us and with us, and we can trust He is faithful.

PRAYER

Dear Lord, thank You for the intricately woven masterpiece of Your Word. Thank You for inspiring every word. Each time we read the scriptures, Your words nourish us and work in us ... deep within our souls. Open our eyes to see Your miraculous provision for us through Christ as we read about Your miraculous provision for the children of Israel. Keep us from grumbling, Lord; fill us each day with joy and gratitude for Your faithfulness. In Jesus' name, amen.

WEEK FIVE

DAY *twenty-one*

SCRIPTURE READING: Exodus 17:8- 18:27

MAJOR MOMENT: Israel defeated Amalek, and Jethro gave his advice.

God had taken His children to places of desperate need so they might know He was the Lord their God. (Exodus 16:12) But the next challenge was different. This time, they would have to fight for themselves: *"Then Amalek came and fought with Israel ..."* (Exodus 17:8). Amalek and his army were descendants of Esau (Jacob's brother). Jacob (whom God renamed "Israel") stole Esau's birthright and blessing from their father, Jacob. This family feud spanned more than 400 years. Amalek hated Israel and saw a chance for revenge.

Amalek knew his men were ready for battle and Israel was not. As re-told in Deuteronomy 25:17-18, Amalek had no fear of God, and knowing that Israel's most vulnerable people would be at the rear of the camp, the Amalekites began their siege by attacking the helpless of Israel.

- According to Exodus 17:9, what steps did Moses rapidly take to prepare Israel?

- Why might Moses have taken the *"staff of God"* with him to the top of the hill? (Exodus 4:2-5; 7:20; 14:15-16)

- Why do you think the Israelites prevailed when Moses' arms were raised?

- _____ and _____ helped Moses. (Exodus 17:12)
  Why do you think their support was necessary for victory?

Bible scholars agree that both Joshua and Moses are representations of Jesus in this passage. Matthew Henry commented: "No doubt it was a great encouragement for the people to see Joshua before them in the field of battle and Moses above them upon the top of the hill: Christ is both to us—our Joshua, the captain of our salvation who fights our battles, and our Moses, who, in the upper world, ever lives making intercession, that our faith fail not." [1]

- How has Jesus been a Joshua and/or Moses to you? (1 John 4:4; Hebrews 7:25)

It was common in biblical times for an altar or memorial to be built after a great military victory to honor the leader of the forces.

- What is the significance of Moses making an altar to God (rather than to Joshua) and naming it *"The Lord Is My Banner?"* (Exodus 17:15-16)

Sometime after the battle with Amalek, Moses' father-in-law traveled from Midian to the desert to visit Moses. Jethro brought Moses' wife and two sons (who had likely been sent to Midian either before or during the exodus). As Jethro listened to Moses share all that God had done to help and provide for His people ... all the miracles ... Jethro's heart was turned toward God.

- How do the words and actions of Jethro in Exodus 18:10-12 express his belief in the Lord?

Jethro witnessed the heaviness and magnitude of Moses' daily responsibilities, and he made some recommendations to Moses. John Calvin gives further insight into Jethro's recommendation: "Jethro made the limitation, that he did not wish his counsel to be obeyed unless God should approve of it." [2]

- What was Moses' response to Jethro's proposal? (Exodus 18:24-26) How was his response an example of a humble and responsible leader?

DAY twenty-two

SCRIPTURE READING: Exodus 19:1-25

MAJOR MOMENT: The Israelites set up camp at Mt. Sinai.

Three months after leaving Egypt, God led the Israelites to the wilderness of Sinai, and they camped in front of the mountain. This mountain was significant because it was the same location where God first appeared to Moses through the burning bush. At that time, Moses was shepherding his father-in-law's flock of sheep; now Moses was shepherding tens of thousands of people (for his Heavenly Father), the nation of Israel.

- Read Exodus 3:9-12 and note all that God had done to fulfill His promise and bring Moses back to this mountain.

In Exodus 19, God reinforced His love for His people by extending to them the proposal of His covenant. Covenant language was God's language of love and commitment. Reminding Israel of the grace and tenderness of His deliverance, (Exodus 19:4) He told them of His desire to make them His *"treasured possession among all the peoples."* Other nations were known for their intellect, military might or wealth; Israel would be known for their God — the One whose presence was evident, whose provision was abundant, and whose protection was constant.

- God's conditions for Israel were: *"if you will indeed _____ my voice and _____ my covenant, you shall be my _____ among all peoples, for all the earth is _____ ; and you shall be to me a kingdom of priests and a holy nation"* (Exodus 19:5-6). How do these verses speak of God's love for Israel?

HOW DO I GET THROUGH THIS?

The priests had access to God; they represented the people to God and God to the people.

- Compare verses 5-6 with 1 Peter 2:9. How is our role today in God's Kingdom similar to the Israelites' role 2,000 years ago?

Israel would be set apart for God, and their obedience would lead to blessing. John Wesley explained: "All the Israelites, if compared with other people, were priests unto God, so near were they to him, so much employed in his immediate service, and such intimate communion they had with him." [3]

Moses went up the mountain to communicate the answer of the people to God and returned with another message from God.

- In Exodus 19:10-11, God told Moses to "_____ *them today and tomorrow and let them wash their garments and* _____ _____ *for the third day."*

- What might be the significance of having clean clothes for this occasion?

God also set specific boundaries around the mountain lest the people be tempted to come too near. The holiness of God was apparent and palpable to the people.

- Compare the boundaries God set for Israel in Exodus 19:12-13 with our freedom of access to God in Hebrews 4:16.

- Why are we able to approach this same God confidently and without fear? (Hebrews 10:19-22)

The morning of the third day, Moses led the people out of the camp to the mountain to meet the Lord. They heard the sounds of thunder and a loud trumpet; they saw flashes of lightning even through the thick cloud that covered the mountain; they felt the earth tremble violently beneath them. Then the Lord descended upon the mountain in fire and called Moses to come up.

DAY *twenty-three*

SCRIPTURE READING: Exodus 20:1-17

MAJOR MOMENT: God gave the Ten Commandments to His people.

The people of Israel saw the Lord's power, felt His presence and heard His voice as He spoke His laws from the midst of the fire. In John Wesley's words, "Never was there such a sermon preached before or since, as this, which was here preached to the church in the wilderness, for the preacher was God himself." [4]

The Ten Commandments were not merely a set of rules; they were evidence of God's love. As a good parent establishes boundaries for the protection of their children, God, as their Father, established boundaries in the same way for the protection and security of His people.

The 10 laws of God fell into two categories: 1) how to love God (commands 1-4), and 2) how to love others (commands 5-10).

- In Exodus 20:2, God reminded Israel of His faithfulness: *"I am the _____ your _____, who _____ you out of the land of Egypt, out of the house of slavery."*

Commandment 1: "You shall have no other gods before me" (v. 3). The Lord was the one true God, their Redeemer, Savior, Deliverer; and He was to be their only God.

- In Matthew 4:10, how did Jesus use this commandment to rebuke Satan?

Commandment 2: "You shall not make for yourself a carved image, or any likeness of anything..." (vv. 4-6). The Lord was the only one worthy of their honor and worship.

- What were the characteristics of the idols of the Old Testament? (Jeremiah 10:3-4)

Commandment 3: "You shall not take the name of the LORD your God in vain" (v. 7). God's name (Yahweh) was sacred, holy and was not even spoken by many in ancient times out of reverence. How do you protect the honor of God's name?

Commandment 4: "Remember the Sabbath day to keep it holy" (vv. 8-11). As God Himself rested from His work of creation on the seventh day, His people were to set aside the Sabbath as a day of rest and worship. How might God's model of the Sabbath influence our own weeks?

Commandment 5: "Honor your father and mother" (v. 12). How are we encouraged to continue respecting and obeying our parents elsewhere in Scripture? See Ephesians 6:1.

Commandment 6: "You shall not commit murder" (v. 13). God created life; man was not to disrespect human life. What does Jesus say about murder in Matthew 5:21-22?

Commandment 7: "You shall not commit adultery" (v. 14). God ordained marriage and the people were to be faithful to their spouses. See Jesus' words in Matthew 5:27-28.

Commandment 8: "You shall not steal" (v. 15). How did Paul rephrase commands 6-10 in Romans 13:9?

Commandment 9: "You shall not bear false witness against your neighbor" (v. 16). God's people were to be a people of truth, not lies. What does Psalm 51:6 say God delights in?

Commandment 10: "You shall not covet…anything that is your neighbor's" (v. 17). They were to be content with God's provision and not desire anything of their neighbors.

- Jesus, the only human to perfectly obey all the commandments, summed up all of the laws in just 28 words. According to Matthew 22:37-40, what were those words?

DAY twenty-four

SCRIPTURE READING: Exodus 20:18-21

MAJOR MOMENT: The people were afraid of God's presence.

According to Exodus 20:18, the people of God, recognizing His mighty power and majesty, were overwhelmed with fear. Before hearing the words spoken by God, they had been tempted to come too close to the mountain, but after all they had seen and heard, they backed away in fear.

- According to verse 19, what did they request of Moses? Why?

Seeing their withdrawal, Moses said, *"Do not fear, for God has come to test you, that the fear of Him may be before you, that you may not sin"* (Exodus 20:20). The two words, "fear" used in verse 20, are two different words in Hebrew. The word, "fear," in the first phrase means "to be afraid." [5]

- How does Moses use this same word in Exodus 14:13?

- Why were they afraid in Exodus 14:13?

HOW DO I GET THROUGH THIS?

The Hebrew word for "fear" in the phrase, *"that the fear of Him may be before you,"* can also mean "reverence." [6] To rephrase Moses' words in Exodus 20:20, "Don't be afraid of God; but revere Him; be in awe of who He is. For as you revere Him, your heart will turn away from sin."

- This Hebrew word for "fear" (to revere) is also used in Proverbs 1:7. How does this give insight to Moses' words to Israel?

The people backed away, but Moses *"drew near to the thick darkness where God was"* (Exodus 20:21). What do you imagine the people were thinking as they saw Moses go into the thick darkness? Were they thinking of the bravery of Moses, or were they thinking that he might not survive?

The difference between the people of Israel and Moses was that Moses chose faith over fear. Moses knew he could trust God, and he was ready to listen to His voice, obey His commands and be His spokesman.

- Write your observations as you compare Moses, the mediator between the Israelites and God, to Jesus Christ, our Mediator before God. Refer to 1 Timothy 2:5 and Hebrews 9:15.

- Give an example in your own life of choosing faith over fear because of knowing Jesus. How did your faith in Him encourage your heart to move forward?

In John 14:21, Jesus told His disciples, *"Whoever has my commandments and keeps them, he it is who loves me. And he who loves me will be loved by my Father, and I will love him and manifest myself to him."* Jesus uses the word "love" four times. This word "love" in the Greek is *agapao:* meaning "true/unconditional love."

- According to John 14:21, explain the relationship between love and obedience.

- How does the covenant of which Jesus spoke apply to us as His disciples today?

DAY *twenty-five*

SCRIPTURE READING: Exodus 20:22-23:19

MAJOR MOMENT: God revealed the details of the law and ordained three feasts.

At the end of Exodus 20, God drew Moses back into the thick darkness on Mount Sinai in order to begin the process of revealing the specific interpretations of the Ten Commandments (later to be called the Book of the Covenant in Exodus 24:7). These laws, spoken directly from the mouth of the Lord, would be used to govern the people and give them guidance in daily life. God also gave them instructions for proper worship.

- According to Exodus 20:23, what did God specifically prohibit? This will become more clear further on in our study, but why might this be an obviously good prohibition?

Chapters 21, 22 and beginning of Chapter 23 in Exodus are filled with specifics of the laws relating to commands 6-10 regarding personal relationships, property rights, treatment of strangers and care of widows and orphans. The Lord set these boundaries over His people to teach them how to live as image-bearers of the One who created them.

According to Exodus 22:29, the Lord reminded Israel that the first fruits of the harvest were His and *"the _____ you shall give to me."* The firstborn sons were to be set apart for Him as holy. Holiness was always God's purpose and plan for His people, and His laws were to help them achieve that purpose.

In Exodus 23:14-19, God gave specific instructions on three feasts to be celebrated by the people. The feasts were to be times of celebration, but also times of remembrance and worship so that Israel would continually trust in His faithfulness throughout all of their generations. The three feasts set aside for the Lord were as follows:

- Feast of _____ _____ (v. 15): to be celebrated immediately following the Passover. They were to eat unleavened bread for seven days in remembrance of their deliverance (in haste) from Egypt.

- Feast of the _____ (v. 16): to be celebrated seven weeks after Passover, this feast would mark the giving of the covenant in the wilderness. It would eventually be called the "Feast of Weeks," and also "Pentecost" because it was 50 days after the Feast of Unleavened Bread.

- Feast of _____ (v. 16): to be celebrated in the fall after they gathered in the harvest. It would later be called the "Feast of Booths" or the "Feast of Tabernacles."

These feasts were also a foreshadowing of another great feast that God's people will celebrate one day. This feast, prepared by God Himself, will be called *"the marriage supper (feast) of the Lamb"* (Revelation 19:9). At this eternal feast, the faithful of God will gather and remember His faithfulness, mercy and love, and we will worship and celebrate the Lamb of God around the table of the King — forever.

WEEKEND REFLECTIONS

As we reflect over the last week, we are reminded of God's faithfulness and commitment to His people every step of the way from Egypt to the promised land. The children of Israel had been freed in order to serve Him, but they were still full of doubts and fears. We are reminded of all that God did for them: He fought for them in the defeat of Amalek; He led them through the pillar of cloud and fire to Mt. Sinai, where He called them His *"treasured possession;"* He established laws and ordinances that they might live in a right relationship with Him and in harmony with each other; and He ordained feasts for them to remember His faithfulness. All of this He did in order to make them His people and bless them because He loved them.

There are seasons of our lives that are much like the desert wilderness. The circumstances of our lives often cause doubts and fears. We need to remember that God has chosen us and called us to be His children so that we can serve Him. He fights for us, He leads and guides us, He provides for us and He gave His only Son, Jesus, to bring us into relationship with Him and set us free from the curse of the law.

God loves us so much. We are now *"a people for His own possession"* (1 Peter 2:9). As we walk in faith and obedience with Him each day, we experience the blessing of knowing Him. We can trust His faithfulness to lead us one day at a time on this earth — until that day when He brings us safely to our eternal home with Him.

John Newton's words in his great hymn, "Amazing Grace," come to mind as we remember Israel's journey so many years ago — and as we travel our journey today:

> "Through many dangers, toils, and snares, I have already come,
> 'Tis grace hath brought me safe thus far,
> And grace will lead me home." [7]

PRAYER

Dear Lord, thank You for the picture of our lives that we see in the lives of the Israelites. Thank You that You are the same yesterday, today and forever. We bow our hearts in worship for who You are and for all that You have done. Thank You that because of Jesus, we can come into Your presence with confidence, clothed in His righteousness. Let us be eager to *"proclaim the excellencies of Him who called us out of darkness into His marvelous light"* (1 Peter 2:9). In Jesus' name, amen.

WEEK SIX

DAY *twenty-six*

SCRIPTURE READING: Exodus 23:20-24:18

MAJOR MOMENT: Canaan was promised, and the covenant was confirmed.

In today's reading, we see three ways God provided for His people as they pressed on through their journey. First, in Exodus 23:20-22, God promised to send an angel before them to guide them to the promised land.

- In Exodus 23:20-23, what did God say the angel would do for His people?

- How did these actions reflect God's character?

- Did God keep His promise? Read Joshua 5:13-15 to find your answer.

- How have you seen God provide protection and direction for you in challenging times?

Second, in Exodus 23:23-33, God warned His people about the spiritual danger they would face in their conquest of the promised land.

- What did God command in Exodus 23:23-33 regarding the people living in the land He would give them?

- While this is shocking for us to read today, what reason did God give for the destruction of these nations? (Exodus 23:33)

As believers living in the 21st century, God calls us to live in the world and yet not conform to the world. Read Romans 12:2 and 1 John 2:15-16.

- How does the world today serve as a snare to believers?

- In which ways are you tempted to love and conform to the ways of this world?

Finally, in Exodus 24, God confirmed His covenant with His people. Moses connected the altar and the people with the blood, depicting the joining of God and the Israelites in the covenant. [1] Despite the people's eagerness to obey the entire law, God knew they would fall short. As His people pledged their obedience, God had already provided a way for their sins to be atoned for and forgiven through the blood of a sacrifice. [2]

Like the Israelites in the wilderness, we have the desire to obey God, but we cannot perfectly keep His commands. (Romans 3:23) Read Luke 22:19-20.

- How has God established a new covenant with us? Whose blood was shed for the forgiveness of your sins?

When the Israelites first gathered at Mt. Sinai, God told Moses to not let the people touch the mountain or come up to try to see the Lord or they would die. (Exodus 19:12, 21) And yet, here in Exodus 24, Moses, Aaron, Nadab, Abihu and 70 elders were permitted to see God, at least in some sense. We are informed in 1 John 4:12 that no one has ever truly seen God. Several times in the Bible, we read that God has allowed people to behold a likeness of Him that allows those around to understand they are meeting with the person of God.

- What is most striking to you about the account of these men and their visit with God?

As we read about this meal on the mountain with God, it should remind us of the glorious future we have in Christ. One day, we will feast at the wedding supper of the Lamb. (Revelation 19:9) Those who have been redeemed through the new covenant in Christ's blood will behold God and eat and drink in His presence.

DAY twenty-seven

SCRIPTURE READING: Exodus 25:1-31:18

MAJOR MOMENT: Many laws for worship were given.

Throughout today's reading, we see a repeated phrase: *"the LORD said to Moses"* (Exodus 25:1, 30:11, 17, 22, 34; 31:1). God gave Moses additional instructions for the people, and they were to be carried out exactly as the Lord commanded.

- Read Exodus 24:18 and Exodus 31:18. Where was Moses? How long was he there? What happened during that time?

- How does it impact your view of God's law to realize that God spoke all these words to Moses and wrote on stone tablets with His finger? (Exodus 31:18)

In Exodus 20-23, God gave the Israelites the moral and civil law. He told them how to live in relationship with Himself and with other people. In Exodus 25-31, we find a different focus. Let's take a look together.

- By scanning the chapters or using the headings in your Bible, make a list of the topics covered by the instructions in these chapters.

- Summarize the content of God's instructions in one or two sentences.

It may seem strange that God gave such detailed instructions for the construction of the tabernacle and its furnishings. God wanted these instructions followed precisely: *"Exactly as I show you concerning the pattern of the tabernacle, and all of its furniture, so you shall make it"* (Exodus 25:9). We might wonder if God is just being picky!

But when we consider the purpose of the tabernacle, we understand why these instructions are important. The Creator of the universe, the almighty God, their Deliverer, was coming to dwell in their midst. (Exodus 25:8)

This is why the Lord brought His people out of Egypt: so that He could dwell with them, and they could serve and worship Him. (Exodus 29:45-46) The Lord is the One worthy of our worship, and He rightly gives commands about how His people worship Him.

- Read Exodus 28:29-30 and 1 Peter 2:24-25. What is the connection here between Aaron and Jesus?

- Just like the Israelites, you've been set apart to serve and worship your Deliverer. How can you respond to the salvation you've received with service and worship today?

DAY twenty-eight

SCRIPTURE READING: Exodus 32:1-14

MAJOR MOMENT: The people worshipped a golden calf.

While Moses was on the mountain for 40 days and 40 nights receiving the law from God, the scene in Exodus 32 shifts to the Israelites who were left under the leadership of Aaron and Hur. The people's path to grave acts of idolatry and false worship started with what *seemed* like a small, insignificant sin. [3]

- Read Exodus 32:1. What concern of the people started the chain of actions that led to the golden calf? How did this show their lack of trust in the Lord?

- Think of a time when your impatience with the Lord's timing caused you to sin. How could you have handled the situation differently?

HOW DO I GET THROUGH THIS?

When the people grew impatient, they also became forgetful. Read the psalmist's description of the golden calf incident in Psalm 106:19-23.

- Think back over the events of Exodus so far. What had the Israelites seen and experienced in Egypt, at the Red Sea, in the wilderness and at Mt. Sinai? What did they know about the Lord? What had He promised to do for them?

- What have you seen and experienced in your life that demonstrates God's mercy, deliverance, power and faithfulness?

- What can you do the next time you're struggling to remember God's deliverance and His promises?

The Israelites' impatience and forgetfulness led to disobedience and idolatry. Even though Moses had not returned with the stone tablets, the people knew God's law and had promised to obey it. (Exodus 24:3) Theologians disagree about whether the Israelites broke the first, second and/or third commandments. But it's clear that their request of Aaron, and Aaron's compliance, broke their covenant with God.

Exodus 32:6 tells us that the people offered burnt offerings and peace offerings, and they ate, drank and played. This counterfeit feast day was a cheap imitation of true worship. It resembled the covenant confirmation ceremony described in Exodus 24:3-11. But the people abandoned the one true God and chased after gods of their own making. [4]

When I read about the Israelites' disobedience, I think, *How could they?* I like to think that if I had been there, I would never have fallen that far. But in 1 Corinthians 10, Paul helps us see ourselves in the Israelites. He wants us to know we're no better — we're also prone to impatience, forgetfulness, disobedience and idolatry.

- Read Paul's comments on this incident in 1 Corinthians 10:6-12. How can the Israelites and the golden calf serve as an example for you?

- How have you set up idols to worship in place of the living God who has delivered you?

As idolatrous sinners, we need a mediator to plead our case before our holy, righteous God. Just as God sent Moses down the mountain to the rebellious Israelites, (Exodus 32:7) God sent His Son to humble Himself, take on human flesh to die for rebellious people like you and me. (Romans 5:8; Philippians 2:6-8)

DAY *twenty-nine*

SCRIPTURE READING: Exodus 32:15-35

MAJOR MOMENT: Moses interceded, and God still sent a plague.

In the passage we read today, the Israelites suffered the consequences of their sin. The Lord decided not to completely destroy His people. (Exodus 32:14) But they still endured consequences, and this served as an important reminder for them — and us — of the seriousness of sin.

When Moses and Joshua arrived at the foot of the mountain, Moses burned with righteous anger and threw the tablets of the testimony down in the same place where the people promised to obey. (Exodus 24:3-8; 32:19) This symbolized the broken relationship between God and the people who failed to keep His covenant. [5]

Next, Moses destroyed the golden calf. He left no chance for the Israelites to return to the worship of this graven image and continue in their disobedience.

- Think back to the idols you identified yesterday. These idols may not be an object that can be ground into powder. But maybe you need to delete an app from your phone, avoid a certain place or a specific crowd, or find someone to hold you accountable for your behavior. Pray and ask God how you can destroy your idols' influence over your heart, your mind, your time and your worship. Write down your next step here.

In Exodus 32:21-24, Moses confronted Aaron.

- What did Aaron get right as he recounted the events of Exodus 32:1-6? Comparing Exodus 32:4 with Exodus 32:24, what did he lie about?

- Just as Adam and Eve did in the garden, Aaron shifted the blame and denied his own wrongdoing. (Genesis 3:12-13) Think back on the last time someone confronted you about your sin. Did you make excuses, or did you confess and repent? What changes do you need to make to accept future rebuke or correction with humility and repentance?

In Exodus 32:25-29, we read about the Levites killing 3,000 men. When we encounter these difficult passages, we need to keep God's character at the forefront of our minds. Exodus 12:37 tells us that thousands of men, women and children were included in the exodus from Egypt. Exodus 32:3 mentions that *"all the people"* brought their gold to Aaron. And yet, not all the people died for their sin.

- What does this tell you about God's holiness, justice and mercy?

In the final verses of this chapter, Moses returned to the Lord and tried to atone for the sin of the people.

- How many times do you see the word "sin" or "sinned" in Exodus 32:30-35? What do you learn from Moses' example of honesty and openness about what happened in the Israelite camp?

- What did Moses offer in Exodus 32:32? What was God's answer?

- Moses did not give his life to secure forgiveness for the people's sin, but we have a Savior who did. Read 1 Peter 2:22 and 1 John 3:5. How was Jesus qualified to atone for our sin?

DAY *thirty*

SCRIPTURE READING: Exodus 33:1-11

MAJOR MOMENT: The Israelites mourned with repentance, and God met with Moses.

In today's reading, the fallout from the incident with the golden calf continued. The Israelites' sin had separated them from God, and the future of God's relationship with His people was still unknown.

- Read Exodus 33:1-3 with Exodus 23:20-23. What remained the same regarding God's promise to the Israelites?

- In Exodus 33:4-6, how did the people respond to the news that God wasn't going with them to the promised land?

When *"the people of Israel stripped themselves of their ornaments"* in Exodus 33:6, this was an act of humility and repentance. Taking off the jewelry that contributed to their sin in Exodus 32:2-3 showed that they were turning from their sin of idolatry. [6]

- What temptation to sin do you need to strip yourself of? How can you take it off and leave it off, showing true repentance in humility before the Lord?

Even though the people were mourning and distressed, there was still hope. Moses still spoke with God in the tent of meeting outside the camp.

- How does Exodus 33:11 say that the Lord spoke with Moses?

God told Moses in Exodus 33:20 that no one can see God's face and live. So we know that when Exodus 33:11 says Moses spoke with God *"face to face,"* this is an expression for their direct conversation. The way Moses spoke with God foreshadowed the way man would one day interact with God's Son, Jesus Christ.

Just as God came down to speak with Moses in the pillar of cloud, the Son of God came down to take on flesh, walk and talk with people, call them to repentance and lay down His life for them.

- Read Romans 5:7-11. How can those who were once God's enemies now become His friends?

- Read John 15:12-17. What do Jesus' words teach us about how we should respond now that we have been redeemed and enjoy friendship with God?

Because Jesus took the punishment for stiff-necked sinners like you and me, we now enjoy God's presence with us through the gift of the Holy Spirit. (Romans 8:11) When we wonder how we will get through tough circumstances, we can have confidence that Jesus will never leave us or forsake us. (Hebrews 13:5) We are more than friends — we are children of God, brought into His family through Jesus's sacrifice. (Romans 8:14-16)

WEEKEND REFLECTIONS

Once again, following along with the Exodus adventures of the Israelites has taken us on a roller coaster ride. We saw the hopeful optimism displayed by the people as they stood at the foot of Mount Sinai and promised to obey. Less than 40 days later, their determination dissolved into disobedience and idolatry.

As Romans 6:23 teaches, disobedience leads to death. The Israelites learned that lesson as they saw 3,000 of their fathers, brothers, sons and friends killed by the Lord's command to the Levites. Their sin required the shedding of blood.

We, like the Israelites, may be eager to obey God's commands. But we, like the Israelites, fall short of the obedience God requires. (Romans 3:23) We constantly give the throne of our hearts to the false gods of comfort, control, approval, pride and pleasure. The good news of the gospel is that Jesus Christ shed His blood for the forgiveness of our sins. *"There is therefore now no condemnation for those who are in Christ Jesus"* (Romans 8:1).

PRAYER

Heavenly Father, thank You for sending Your Son to rescue me from the endless cycle of sin and shame. I confess that my heart is prone to wander and chase after idols. Thank You for mercifully forgiving my sin. By the power of Your Spirit, help me to keep seeking You and growing in obedience to Your Word. In Jesus' name, amen.

WEEK SEVEN

DAY *thirty-one*

SCRIPTURE READING: Exodus 33:12-34:28

MAJOR MOMENT: God through Moses wrote the Ten Commandments again.

In this passage, we are taken inside the tent and onto the mountain to witness God's conversations with His servant Moses. In these encounters, we'll find hope for God's weary people who are ready to give up and walk away from His plan.

- What three things did Moses ask of God in Exodus 33:12-23? How did God respond?

- From Exodus 33:16, why was it so important to Moses that God went with the Israelites?

God granted Moses' request to go with the Israelites not because He was pleased with the Israelites but because He was pleased with Moses. (Exodus 33:17) Moses' role as a mediator points us to our Lord Jesus Christ.

- Read Matthew 3:17. What does the Father say about the Son?

- Read 2 Corinthians 5:21. In what way is Jesus an even better mediator than Moses?

- Have you placed your faith in Christ to be your Savior and your mediator before God? If so, you have been forgiven and declared righteous. Write a prayer of thanksgiving and praise to your Redeemer.

Moses had several close encounters with God before this one: at the burning bush; on the mountain with Aaron, his sons and the elders; on Mount Sinai when God gave Moses the law and in the tent of meeting outside the camp. And yet, Moses had not yet seen all there was to see of God's glory.

- In Exodus 33:11, we're told Moses spoke to God *"face to face."* However, remember from last week that based on this verse and others like it, (John 1:18; 4:14) we know that no one has truly ever fully *seen* God except God the Son. "Face to face" is a way of expressing the personal way Moses was able to communicate with God. What does it teach us about God's character that not even Moses could see God's face and live? (Exodus 33:20)

- As the Lord passed by Moses and proclaimed His name, what do we learn about Him? How did Moses respond to this revelation?

- Read John 1:14-18. How has God shown us His glory and made Himself known to us? How will you respond today?

God's mercy, grace, love and faithfulness are on brilliant display in these verses. We see these traits in God's proclamation of His name and in His care for His people. God accepted Moses as the mediator for the Israelites. He continued His presence with the rebellious people. He rewrote the stone tablets that Moses broke. And God granted Moses' request to see His glory while protecting Moses in the cleft of the rock.

God shows the same mercy, grace, love and faithfulness to us today. He has revealed Himself to us in His Word and in His Son, Jesus Christ. He has given One who is an even better mediator than Moses — Jesus, our perfect Redeemer. He has written His law on our hearts and given us the indwelling Holy Spirit. Because of Christ, we know that nothing in all creation will be able to separate us from the love of God. (Romans 8:38-39)

DAY *thirty-two*

SCRIPTURE READING: Exodus 34:29-35

MAJOR MOMENT: The face of Moses shone brightly.

In this passage, we are taken inside the tent and onto the mountain to witness God's conversations In Exodus 34:29, Moses descended after his fourth trip up Mount Sinai to meet with God. He had the two replacement tablets, and he was ready to relay the instructions God gave while the people were busy making a golden calf. But there was a problem Moses wasn't aware of: His face was shining, and the people were terrified. (Exodus 34:30)

According to a commentary by Philip Graham Ryken, the phrase in these verses that says *"the skin of his face shone"* could be literally translated as "the skin of his face sent out horns." [1] The expression doesn't mean horns like an animal, but rays of light. As Ryken said, "Dazzling beams of light were shining out from his face." [2] Can you imagine?

- What does Exodus 34:29 tell us about why Moses's face was shining?

- When did Moses wear the veil, and when did he take it off?

- What does the fear of the people and the need for Moses to wear a veil teach you about God's glory?

Take a moment to read 2 Corinthians 3:7-18 carefully. Paul gives us a commentary on Exodus 34. He compares the old covenant God made with Moses to the new covenant we have in Christ.

- Using 2 Corinthians 3:7-11, fill in the blanks in the chart below.

	MINISTRY OF…	GLORY	DURATION
Old Covenant	1. Death 2. Condemnation	Lesser glory	Brought to an end
New Covenant	1. the _____ (v.8) 2. _____ (v.9)	_____ (v.10)	_____ (v.11)

Now let's look at 2 Corinthians 3:12-18. We'll see why this new covenant in Christ fills us with hope and boldness.

- According to 2 Corinthians 3:14, 16, what part do we play in the veil being removed from our face? Who removes the veil?

- Look at 2 Corinthians 3:18. When we behold the glory of the Lord with an unveiled face, what is the result? Who brings about this result in our lives?

- Read Romans 8:29. Whose image are we being transformed into?

The glory Moses reflected caused dazzling beams to come out of his face. The glory we behold in Jesus Christ is even greater, and it never fades. And it gets even better! We are being conformed to the image of Christ, who is *"the radiance of the glory of God"* (Hebrews 1:3). Moses reflected God's glory, but we have the privilege of resembling the Lord Jesus Christ. And not so others might cower before God's glory in fear, but that they might see the light of Christ's love in our lives, turn to Him and have their own veil removed.

DAY *thirty-three*

SCRIPTURE READING: Exodus 35:1-3

MAJOR MOMENT: Moses repeated the regulations about the Sabbath day.

Exodus 35:1 serves as an introduction to the final chapters of the book, which describe how the people carried out God's commands to build and erect the tabernacle. [3] As we continue our study of these chapters, we will see how important it was that everything was done exactly as the Lord commanded them.

As the people began the work, Moses told them the first rule of tabernacle construction: The work must cease on the Sabbath.

The Sabbath was first introduced in Exodus 16 when the people started receiving manna. They were commanded to collect twice as much on the sixth day, because the seventh day would be "*... a day of solemn rest, a holy Sabbath to the* LORD *...*" (Exodus 16:23). The Hebrew word for sabbath is *shabbat*, which means "cease" or "desist." [4] The people were to cease working and trust God's provision.

- How would you describe your view of the Sabbath? Do you view it as an Old Testament tradition that is no longer relevant? A command to be strictly followed? Is it a day of leisure, a day for catching up on work or a day filled with church-related activities?

- Is it difficult for you to cease working and rest? If so, why do you think this is a struggle for you?

After the Sabbath was commanded in Exodus 20:8-11, God gave Moses an expanded explanation of the Sabbath in Exodus 31:12-17.

- Fill in the blanks from these verses that list the reasons God gave for the Sabbath.

"... this is a _____ _____ _____ _____ _____

throughout your generations, that you may know that I, the Lord, sanctify you" (Exodus 31:13).

"... it is _____ for you" (Exodus 31:14).

"it is a sign _____ between me and the people of Israel that in six days the Lord made heaven and earth, and on the seventh day he _____ and was _____" (Exodus 31:17).

When Moses summarizes God's commands about the Sabbath here in Exodus 35:1-3, we see one interesting addition. Exodus 35:3 commands the people to not even start a fire in their homes.

- What would kindling a fire enable the people to do on the Sabbath? Why do you think God specifically forbade it?

In the Gospels, we learn more about the Sabbath from Jesus. (For further study, see Luke 4:16, Luke 13:10-17 and John 5:1-17.)

Read Mark 2:23-3:6.

- How did Jesus' view of the Sabbath differ from that of the Pharisees?

- What do you think Jesus meant in Mark 2:27 when He said, *"The Sabbath was made for man, not man for the Sabbath"*?

Friend, the Sabbath is not a burden, a litmus test of our spirituality, or another opportunity to prove ourselves. It is a gracious gift from our good Shepherd.

- What changes do you need to make in your attitude toward the Sabbath to rightly enjoy the gift of rest that God has given you?

DAY thirty-four

SCRIPTURE READING: Exodus 35:4-29

MAJOR MOMENT: Moses gave instructions regarding offerings.

The first step in any building project is to gather the necessary materials. The same was true for the construction of the tabernacle. God gave very specific commands about how the tabernacle and its furnishings were to be made. (Exodus 25-31) The Israelites were former slaves wandering in the wilderness, so where would they find these materials?

- Read Exodus 12:33-36. Where did the Israelites' possessions come from?

- Why were they able to successfully plunder the Egyptians?

After Moses gave his call to the congregation to bring their possessions and their skills, Exodus 35:20 tells us that the entire congregation left. Imagine for a moment the scene in the wilderness as the people disappeared into their tents and returned with this brilliant array of supplies.

- What did the people bring to Moses? Make a list from Exodus 35:22-28.

- Read through Exodus 35:20-29 and note each time the text says "every" or "all." How was this a group effort?

- Then read through Exodus 35:20-29 again and note each time the text says "everyone who possessed . . ." or "everyone who could . . ." How was this an individualized effort?

- In Exodus 35:20-29, what repeated phrase describes the people's motivation for bringing their offering?

Different people possessed different resources and skills. God, in His sovereignty, ensured that when all the individual contributions came together, His people had everything they needed.

- How has the Lord blessed you with possessions, wealth or resources you can use to serve Him and build His Kingdom?

- How has the Lord stirred your heart today, and how will you respond?

From a wandering crowd of former slaves, God provided everything they needed to keep His commands and build the tabernacle. We know from Philippians 4:19 that God will meet all our needs, and we can trust Him to keep this promise because of the riches of His glory. No matter what seemingly impossible task the Lord calls you to, you can depend on Him to supply everything you need.

- Are there ways in which you feel ill-equipped to do what God is asking you to do?

- What difference would it make to trust God to provide everything you need to serve Him and follow His commands?

DAY thirty-five

SCRIPTURE READING: Exodus 35:30-36:7

MAJOR MOMENT: Moses instructed the people on who was to build the tabernacle.

Can you feel the excitement mounting? The supplies were ready, and the construction of the tabernacle was almost ready to begin. God gave detailed, specific instructions for the tabernacle and its furnishings. I wonder if the Israelites looked around and wondered: Who could possibly carry out God's plans?

Read Exodus 35:30-36:1 with Exodus 31:1-6.

- What do you learn about God from these verses?

- What do you learn about Bezalel and Oholiab?

- List the gracious gifts God has given to these two men who were called to do this important work.

Bezalel is the first person in the Old Testament who is said to be filled with the Spirit of God. (Exodus 31:3) [5] In the Old Testament, God filled His people with His Spirit to equip them for a task. (See Joshua in Deuteronomy 34:9 and Micah in Micah 3:8.) [6] God knows His people. He calls them to do specific work for His Kingdom, and then He uniquely equips them to carry out His calling.

Read Ephesians 2:19-22. Let's look at how God builds His household today.

- What is the foundation of the household of God? Who is the cornerstone?

- Fill in the blanks to show **who** is being built together into God's dwelling place and **by whom** they are being built together:

"In him _____ *also are being built together into a dwelling place for God by* _____ _____ *"* (Ephesians 2:22).

- What connection to the tabernacle do you see in Ephesians 2:22?

If you are in Christ, God has called you by name to help build His Kingdom. He has equipped you with His Word and His Spirit, along with the skills and knowledge He's given you.

- What role has God called you to play in building His Kingdom in your current location and season of life?

- How can you use the gifts God has given you to serve others in your sphere of influence today?

WEEKEND REFLECTIONS

God didn't ask His people to get through this journey on their own. Throughout this week's passages, we've seen how He provided for His people.

- God provided Moses as a mediator for the Israelites who had broken their covenant with Him.
- God provided a way for the people to hear His instructions through Moses and glimpse a reflection of His glory.
- God provided a day of rest each week known as the Sabbath.
- God provided the resources and the skills the people needed to build the tabernacle.

These examples of God's provision aren't simply God's way of relating to the Israelites many centuries ago. No matter how challenging our journey may be, we can trust God to be our provider today.

- God has given us a mediator, Jesus Christ, who died for our sin, rose again and intercedes for us at the right hand of the Father. (Romans 8:34)
- God has removed the veil from our eyes so we can see His glory in Jesus Christ as we are transformed into Christ's image. (2 Corinthians 3:18)
- God has given us a day to rest and be refreshed by worship, His Word and fellowship with other believers in our local church.
- God has promised to make His all-sufficient grace abound in our lives so we can do the work He's called us to do. (2 Corinthians 9:8)

Let's rejoice today in the provision of our faithful Father!

PRAYER

Thank You, Heavenly Father, for being my perfect Provider. I am needy and often blind to what I truly need. And yet, in Your wisdom and mercy, You lovingly and faithfully supply everything I need through Your Son, Jesus Christ. Help me to trust You and depend on You for all that I need today. In Jesus' name, amen.

WEEK EIGHT

DAY thirty-six

SCRIPTURE READING: Exodus 36:8-38

MAJOR MOMENT: The tabernacle was constructed.

Now that God's gifted artisans had collected the materials to build the tabernacle, the time had come for the real work to begin. Earlier in Exodus (Exodus 25-27), God gave Moses specific, detailed instructions for design and structure of the tabernacle.

- Read Exodus 25:1-9. What instructions did God give Moses on Mount Sinai?

This week, God repeats those very same instructions, almost word for word, not for design and structure, but for the actual construction of the tabernacle. Why would God repeat every detail again? Though it might seem redundant, it's not. God's repetition of words and instructions tells God's people to stand up and pay attention ... this is important!

Why was God so specific as to the design and construction of the tabernacle?

- The author of Hebrews provides insight in Hebrews 8:5a, *"They serve a _____ and _____ of the heavenly things."*

The tabernacle was an earthly picture of a heavenly reality. Each part and piece revealing prophetic pictures of Jesus.

God's heart has always been to dwell among His people. He dwelled with Adam and Eve in the garden. He then dwelled with them in the tabernacle. God dwelled with them again in the temple. God's desire to be with His people became more evident, more tangible in the New Testament.

- Read John 1:14. As we enter into the New Testament, how did God dwell with His people?

God sent His Son to earth on a rescue mission. Jesus came and literally "dwelt" among His people. The word "dwelt" here is from the Greek word *skénoó,* which means "to have one's tent, place of dwelling, tabernacle." Jesus tabernacled with His people! Jesus' coming reveals that God's dwelling place was no longer restricted to a building.

And, after Jesus' resurrection, God's dwelling place changed again. Jesus still lives among His people but in a new and better way. He lives through His Church. And, again, it's not about the building. He indwells the body of Christ. He lives in the hearts and minds of each and every one of His children who make up His Church.

- Read Ephesians 2:19-22 and 1 Peter 2:4-5, 9. How do these verses speak to what we're learning, and what do they mean to you personally?

THE TABERNACLE AS COSMOS
WHERE GOD AND MANKIND MET

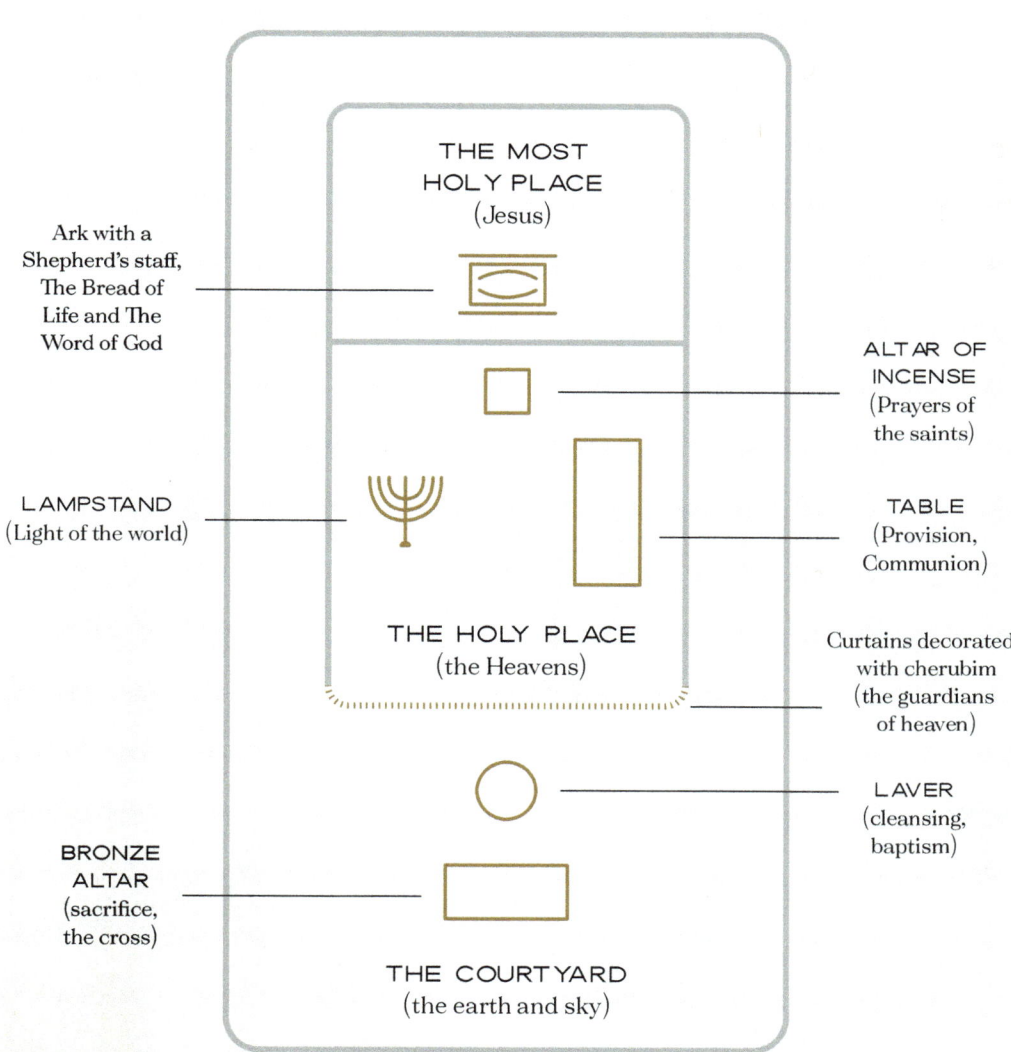

THE TABERNACLE AS A
SYMBOL OF THE COSMOS

The **tabernacle** was a large tent with multiple rooms, and it is full of symbolism. One thing that has been pointed out by scholars is how the tabernacle is a shadow and/or copy of spiritual things in heaven and on earth. (Hebrews 8:5) The ancient Hebrew view of the universe was much different from ours today. Rather than revolving around the sun, the earth is seen more as the center of the universe, with the sun and stars actually moving across our sky. Above these, the sky was literally seen as the lower parts of heaven, and somewhere in that sky was the gate to heaven, the heaven of heavens, where God resided.

Other ancient cultures shared similar views when it came to heaven and earth. Heaven and earth were not totally separate places; the heaven of heavens was simply unreachable according to our human limitations.

The word "cosmos" is a word that is sometimes used to describe all of reality. The cosmos includes both the physical and spiritual worlds together as one. While we have made advances in science and understand our physical universe much better today than ancient cultures did, there may be more truth to how the spiritual and physical worlds are connected than we often realize. The tabernacle is one of the clearest places in Scripture that shows this connection. For 40 years, the Israelites made their homes in tents. As a larger tent, the tabernacle itself represents God's love and attention to humanity, and His intention to *dwell* with humankind on the earth. (Exodus 29:45; Revelation 21:3) Inside the tabernacle then, we see symbolism for the true way that God meets with mankind.

The Courtyard. The **curtains** of the tabernacle were decorated with cherubim. (Exodus 26:1, 31) Cherubim guarded Eden (Genesis 3:24) and guards the throne of God in Ezekiel 10 and Isaiah 6. This embroidery therefore signifies the entrance to heaven, where God dwells. A priest would perform a sacrifice on the bronze **altar**. Sacrifice served as a reminder of sin (Hebrews 10:3) and also to demonstrate that *"without the shedding of blood there is no forgiveness of sins."* (Hebrews 9:22) The priest would wash his hands and feet in the bronze **laver** or basin before entering the Holy Place in order that he would not be killed by God for entering his presence as unclean. (Exodus 30:20)

The Holy Place. Inside the Holy Place, the priests would go regularly to perform their ritual duties with the lampstand, the table and the altar of incense. (Numbers 28:3; Hebrews 9:6) Israelites saw the **lampstand** as representing the sun, moon and stars, the times and the seasons. The **table** holds the bread of the Presence, which was representative of God's overall provision for His creatures. From the heavens God *"... makes his sun rise on the evil and on the good, and sends rain on the just and on the unjust"* (Matthew 5:45). Not only was **incense** an air deodorizer and an insect repellant, [1] but it symbolized authorized worship. (Exodus 30)

Only once a year did a priest enter the **Most Holy Place** after making sacrifices for himself and the unintentional sins of the people. (Hebrews 9:7) Here he prayed and spoke with God, who manifested his presence over the **Ark** and between two carved cherubim. (Exodus 25:22)

All of these things are shadows and copies of heavenly things that are revealed to us in Jesus Christ:

01. THE EARTH AND SKY -
THE COURTYARD

The courtyard of the tabernacle is where any Israelite was allowed. It is a picture of one important way people can find God: Go to where His people are. Today, that place is Christ's body, the Church, the people of God (1 Corinthians 12:27) who may or may not meet in an actual building, tent or temple, but they do meet together. (Hebrews 10:25; 12:23) The bronze **altar** represents the sacrificial cross of Christ and the **laver** represents baptism and the cleansing from sin. Both faith in the cross of Christ's sacrifice, and baptism as an appeal to God for a good conscience, (1 Peter 3:21) are entry points into the family of God. These are the most public aspects of the Church.

02. THE HEAVENS -
THE HOLY PLACE

A person is cleansed from sin not from water but by having faith in Christ and His sacrifice on the cross. This happens before becoming a part of the Church. And the work of Christ in the Church has *"blessed us in Christ with every spiritual blessing in the heavenly places"* (Ephesians 1:3). This is what we see in the Holy Place: There is a real and spiritual sense in which true believers are in this heavenly Holy Place, in a spiritual sense. The Kingdom of God is with His people both now already and not yet fully. (1 John 3:2)

> THE LAMPSTAND. The whole world has always seen God's creation in areas like the heavenly lights, and *"clearly perceived"* God's divine nature so that we are all without excuse for believing in God. (Romans 1:20) In the Psalms, the moon is called a *"witness"* to God's faithfulness through Christ, the everlasting offspring of David. *"Like the moon it shall be established forever, a faithful witness in the skies"* (Psalm 89:37). Today, believers shine like lights in the world, (Matthew 5:16) imitating Jesus, who is the Light of the world. (John 8:12)

> THE TABLE. Just as only a priest could enter the Holy Place, only believers in Christ are instructed to take and eat at God's table during communion. (1 Corinthians 11:29, 1 Peter 2:9)

> THE INCENSE. Like Jesus, and because of Jesus, who *"passed through the heavens"* for us (Hebrews 4:14), our prayers reach God, who delights in the prayers of His people, the Church, and describes our prayers as a pleasing incense. (Psalm 141:2; Revelation 8:4) In

03. JESUS -
AND THE MOST HOLY PLACE

Since it is impossible for the blood of animals to actually take away sins, (Hebrews 10:4, 11) Jesus' life, death and resurrection atoned for our sins once for all time. (Hebrews 10:11-14)

The original high priests also spoke with God in front of the Ark. Jesus Himself is this great High Priest for us. (Hebrews 4:14) The Ark was called the "mercy seat" of God, (Exodus 25:21; Hebrews 9:5) which is like a throne and a "footstool" where God has contact with creation. (1 Chronicles 28:2; Psalms 99:5) Jesus is where God has the most intimate contact with His creation, humanity. *"For in him **the whole fullness** of deity dwells bodily"* (Colossians 2:9, emphasis added). God also now dwells richly in His people (1 Corinthians 6:19; Romans 8:11; 2 Timothy 1:14).

Inside the ark were kept the **tablets** of stone (God's Word), Aaron's **staff** (a Leader's and Shepherd's staff) and the manna (supernatural **bread**). We find out in the New Testament that Jesus Himself is the Word of God, (John 1:1, 14; Revelation 19:13) the Good Shepherd (John 10:11) and the supernatural Bread of Life. (John 6:35)

The tabernacle was a portable temple. The temple, built by Solomon when the Israelites had finally settled in their promised land, was patterned after the tabernacle. The veil in the temple between the Holy Place and the Most Holy Place was torn in two by God after the death of Jesus. (Matthew 27:51) We see Jesus Himself, then, as the true Most Holy Place. Jesus is *"the image of the invisible God"* (Colossians 1:15) and *"the radiance of the glory of God and the exact imprint of his nature ... he upholds the universe by the word of his power"* (Hebrews 1:3). Jesus calls *Himself* the new temple, (John 2:21) and we also know there will be no other temple in heaven but Jesus. (Revelation 21:22) *Jesus* is therefore where His people, the Church, meet with God.

DAY *thirty-seven*

SCRIPTURE READING: Exodus 37:1-9

MAJOR MOMENT: God revealed the design of the veil and the ark.

Today, we enter into the Most Holy Place in the tabernacle. We find it hidden behind a magnificent, colorful, ornate veil. It was in this most holy space God chose to dwell and live among His people.

This veil separated the Holy Place from the Most Holy Place and served as a barrier between God and man. No one except the high priest could enter behind the veil. And, even then, he could only go one time a year on the Day of Atonement to offer a blood sacrifice — a perfect lamb, to cover the sins of God's people. Without the high priest's sacrifice, there was no access to God for anyone, ever, because sin stood in the way.

But then, the moment Jesus took His last breath on the cross, something miraculous happened to this veil.

- Read Matthew 27:50-51. What happened?

Jesus' sacrificial death broke the barrier that stood between God and man. He gave the way back to life that had been cut off in the garden of Eden. Jesus shed His blood once and for all so that we could enter into His presence anytime, anywhere. Hallelujah!

- What does this mean to you personally?

Additionally, behind the veil, we find Israel's greatest treasure, the Ark of the Covenant, which held The Ten Commandments and a few other treasured, holy objects. Atop the ark was a solid gold covering called the mercy seat. This mercy seat was the meeting place of God and sinners.

On the Day of Atonement, the high priest sprinkled blood on the mercy seat. The blood portrayed that God no longer saw the broken law. Instead, He saw the animal's blood, and that blood temporarily covered the sins of God's people and restored their fellowship with Him. (Leviticus 16) The Hebrew word for "atonement" in Leviticus 4:20 is *kaphar*, which means "to cover over." These sacrifices were essentially like a bandage, only acting as a covering for sin. They did not, and could not, remove sin. (Hebrews 10:4)

The Day of Atonement foreshadows Jesus' sacrifice on the cross. In the New Testament, Jesus made a better way. Jesus *became* the mercy seat. The meeting place between God and sinners. When we accept Jesus' blood sacrifice on the cross as forgiveness for our sins, God no longer sees our sin; He sees Jesus' shed blood. We receive a better and greater gift than the Israelites. Jesus' blood doesn't just cover our sin. It erases and eradicates it once and for all.

- Fill in the blanks for 2 Corinthians 5:21. *"For _____ sake he made him to be sin who knew no sin, _____ _____ in him _____ might become the _____ of God."*

Our Savior is not lying dead in a grave. He is now risen and sitting at the right hand of His Father, interceding on our behalf, awaiting His magnificent Second Coming where He will rule and reign. And by His blood, we, who have been made righteous in Jesus, will one day walk through the gates of that heavenly sanctuary to live and reign with Him. (2 Timothy 2:11-12)

- Read what Hebrews 9:24-28 says about the heavenly sanctuary and Jesus' second coming. How many times does the author use the word "appear"? Share what each use means for us as children of God.

- What do the following verses teach about Jesus' return?

    1. John 14:1-3

    2. 1 Corinthians 15:50-57

    3. 1 John 3:2

DAY *thirty-eight*

SCRIPTURE READING: Exodus 37:10-29

MAJOR MOMENT: God revealed the design of the Holy Place and its contents.

Today, we leave the Most Holy Place and enter the Holy Place where we find three pieces of furniture. The first is the only source of light in the Holy Place, the golden lampstand, made of pure gold. It resembled the modern-day Jewish menorah. The craftsmen created a central shaft with six branches extending up and out, three on each side. Each branch adorned with cups shaped like almond blossoms.

- Read Exodus 27:20-21 and Leviticus 24:3-4. What oil did God require? How often did the priest tend the lampstand?

Practically, the lampstand provided light for the priest as he served. But, symbolically and spiritually, the lampstand pointed forward to the coming Messiah.

- Read John 1:6-9 and 8:12. How does the lampstand point to Jesus?

The central shaft represents Christ as the Light of the World. The six branches and the cups represent His followers. That's you and me.

- Read Matthew 5:14-16. Fill in the blanks.

"YOU ARE THE _____ OF THE WORLD. A CITY SET ON A HILL CANNOT BE HIDDEN. NOR DO PEOPLE LIGHT A LAMP AND PUT IT UNDER A BLANKET. BUT ON A STAND, AND IT GIVES LIGHT TO ALL IN THE HOUSE. IN THE SAME WAY, LET _____ LIGHT SHINE BEFORE OTHERS, _____ _____ THEY MAY _____ YOUR GOOD WORKS AND _____ GLORY TO _____ _____ WHO IS IN HEAVEN."

Just as the priests continually filled the almond cups to keep them burning, we too must continually fill ourselves to keep our light shining by spending time with Jesus, soaking in His Word and His presence so He can fill us to overflowing. (John 15:5)

Next, we find the table of showbread (the bread of the Presence). Each Sabbath, the priest placed 12 loaves of bread on the table.

- Why did God choose the number 12? (See Genesis 35:22b-26)

Much about this bread pointed to Jesus. First, God instructed it be baked without leaven, which in Scripture often represents sin. The bread of the Presence depicts the body of our Lord, who was completely sinless.

Then, as the priest broke the bread, this too pointed to Jesus, who would be broken for us. In that brokenness, life poured out. Jesus said, *"I am the living bread that came down from heaven. Whoever eats this bread will live forever. If anyone eats of this bread, he will live forever. And the bread that I will give for the life of the world is my flesh"* (John 6:51).

Finally, we find the altar of incense directly before the veil. Here, the priest offered incense to the Lord, signifying two important things. First, it pointed to Jesus who serves to intercede before the Father on our behalf. It's why we pray in Jesus' name.

- What else did the incense symbolize? (See Revelation 5:8)

Friend, our prayers are ever before the Lord, orchestrating events in the spiritual realm that will one day manifest themselves in the physical realm. So, when you feel as if you can't take another step. Or you want to give up. Bow low before your Father in heaven. Lift your prayers to Him. He is there. He is listening. He is working in and through them.

- How full is your golden bowl of prayers?

DAY thirty-nine

SCRIPTURE READING: Exodus 38

MAJOR MOMENT: God revealed the design of the outer courtyard and its contents.

Today, we leave the inner courtyard and step into the outer courtyard where we find a gate — the one and only entrance to the tabernacle, at the east end. This gate foreshadows Jesus being the one and only way to salvation. (John 14:6)

As we walk through the gate into the outer courtyard, we encounter another altar, the brazen altar. It was here the priest offered sacrifices on behalf of God's people, more specifically a perfect lamb for the sin of the one who brought the lamb.

The brazen altar foreshadows the cross. The blood sacrifices prophesy Jesus who became the perfect Lamb and offered His life for ours as a once and for all final and forever sacrifice.

Read 1 Peter 1:18-19 and Hebrews 10:1-4, 8-10; 11:9-14 to confirm what we learned.

The next piece of furniture we encounter is the laver, a basin filled with water made from highly polished brass mirrors, that stood between the brazen altar and The Holy Place. God's holiness necessitated that before entering the Holy Place, the priest cleanse himself to remove any blood remaining after his sacrificial offerings.

Like the altar, the laver points to Jesus. Though Jesus' blood freed us from the law of sin and death, we, like the priest, need daily cleansing. Both the laver made of mirrors and the water point us to this daily cleansing.

- Read James 1:22-25. What word connects with what we learned about the laver and what does it do when we act upon it?

- Read 2 Timothy 3:16. How does this verse speak to what we've learned about God's Word and its purpose in our lives?

- Read Ephesians 5:25-26, 1 John 1:9 and John 15:3. How do they relate to the laver, our cleansing and the purpose of God's Word?

Just as the laver washed and cleansed the priests to set them apart for service in the tabernacle, God's Word sanctifies (sets apart and makes holy) the children of God to do His Kingdom work. The Word helps us see our sin, cleanses and sanctifies us. The Holy Spirit then empowers us to adjust our actions to continually walk in the light of Jesus' power, mercy and grace.

We also find a larger meaning behind Christ's work in the outer courtyard. The brazen altar speaks of Jesus' death and the laver speaks of His resurrection. Jesus' death justified us, forever removing our sin and making us right with God. Jesus' resurrection ushered in the Holy Spirit's presence and power, making us alive in Christ, regenerating us from the inside out to be a new creation. (John 1:12-13) And, our part comes in the process of sanctification. This is where we intentionally choose to faithfully connect and engage our hearts and minds to God's living and active Word. (Hebrews 4:12) As we do this, the Spirit works to correct and redirect us so we can continually walk in the light and love of Jesus.

DAY forty

SCRIPTURE READING: Exodus 39-40

MAJOR MOMENT: The priestly garments were created, and God's glory fell upon the tabernacle.

Today we study Israel's most significant priestly figure, the high priest, and two of his grand garments, beginning with his outermost garment, the ephod.

- Read Exodus 39:1-7. List the colors in the ephod and what attached the front and back of the ephod at the shoulders.

The high priest's ephod resembled an elaborate apron. Each of its colors foreshadowed the better things to come in Jesus, who is our Great High Priest. White represented Jesus' purity and righteousness. Blue represented our Lord's divinity and heavenly origin. Purple represented Jesus' royalty as the King of kings and Lord of lords. Scarlet represented Jesus' shed blood.

Two onyx stones, engraved with the 12 tribes of Israel, joined the front and back of the ephod at the shoulder. The stones reminded the high priest that he represented and interceded for the people of Israel, just as Jesus represents and intercedes for us today before our heavenly Father.

- We see a phrase repeated in the closing verses of Exodus 39:1b, 5b, 7b. Fill in the blanks: "as the _____ had _____ _____."

- Read Exodus 39:8-21. What similarities do you see in the ephod and the breastpiece? What about the breastpiece's design points to Jesus?

HOW DO I GET THROUGH THIS?

- Read Exodus 28:30. What else do you learn about the breastpiece?

God designed this breastpiece to equip the high priest to seek God's wisdom. The actual workings of the Urim and Thummim remain a mystery. But God made it clear by including them in the design that He wanted to guide His people. His desire to guide and lead continues even today. Thankfully, we no longer have to rely on stones. We have much better ways: God guides through His Word and His Spirit.

- What phrase do we see repeated again in Exodus 39:21, 26, 29, 30 and 32?

The Israelites then brought the completed tabernacle pieces to Moses for his inspection.

- Read verses 42-43. What phrase do you see again? What did Moses do?

What a magnificent day that must have been!

But God had more. He fulfilled His promise when His glory, a visible manifestation of His presence in the form of brilliant light and consuming fire, fell and filled the Most Holy Place. Not even Moses could enter because God's splendor fell so thick and full.

As magnificent as that moment was, Jesus brought more and better. He entered behind the veil and became the true tabernacle.

- Read John 1:14 and 14:16-17. How do these verses speak to what we're studying?

God no longer limited His Presence to indwelling a building.

At Pentecost, His presence fell in a most spectacular way upon the believers gathered in the upper room, filling each one. (Acts 2:1-4)

And God's presence falls again when we invite Jesus to be our Lord and Savior. He comes and fills His church and His people. (1 Corinthians 3:16; 6:19)

Oh, friend, Jesus died for you. Jesus set you free to be free! Free from striving, worry and fear. Free to take hold of His incomparably great power who lives in you and walk confidently and expectantly into that beautiful, peace-filled, grace-saturated freedom!

WEEKEND REFLECTIONS + PRAYER

Let's close our study by reflecting on and praying through God's magnificent tabernacle.

SANCTIFYING

Father, just as the priest came before You at the brazen altar, I come before You today, offering myself as a living sacrifice, holding nothing back. Ignite a fire in my heart and keep it ever burning with a passion for more of You. With every fiber of my being, help me to comprehend how wide and high and deep and long is Your great love for me. And as that love consumes me, help me to love You back, desiring You above all else this world offers. Empower me to die to self and envelop my will in Yours.

CLEANSING

Father, just as the priest washed himself in the laver, wash me with Your Word. Cleanse my heart and renew my mind. And as I look into your living, active, life-transforming Word, give me eyes to see myself as I really am. Rebuke me. Teach me. Mold me. Convict me. Lead me to repentance. By Your love and grace, transform me and restore me. And equip me to live and walk in step with Your Spirit and Your Word.

FILLING

Father, just as the priest stood before the lampstand in the Holy Place, I pause there as well. I know there is no light apart from You. Thank You that no matter how dark it might get, You are brighter still. In You there is no darkness at all! You are the Light of my life and in my life. As the oil filled the almond blossoms, fill me as I meet with You each day. Refresh and renew my Spirit. Fix my eyes on You alone. Fill me to overflowing so I can then pour into others.

STRENGTHENING

Father, as the priest shared in the Bread of the Presence in the Holy Place, I want to feast on You because You alone can satisfy my every need. You are the Bread of Life and You alone are enough. Strengthen me from within as I feast on Your Word. May I not just ingest, but help me to digest each and every morsel. Give me a grateful heart, one sustained by You and You alone. You are the Bread of Heaven that nourishes, sustains and strengthens me. Jesus, I cannot live without You!

INTERCEDING

Father, just as the priest offered the incense at the altar of incense, I come before You offering my prayers. I love that the incense offered in the golden bowls was a pleasing aroma to You. May my prayers be the same. Father, prick my heart to stand in the gap for the broken, the lost, the hopeless, and those in need around me. Give me eyes to see them and a heart of compassion to pray for them. Fill my mouth with Your words so that my prayers will be powerful and effective. Thank You that through my prayers, the eternal pierces the temporal. Use me in that precious and holy place so I can see Your hand at work in unmistakable and indescribable ways! Break strongholds. Loosen chains. Untangle lies. Destroy doubts. Increase faith. Bring salvation. I'm enlisting as a soldier in Your army, Lord. Use me.

THANKSGIVING

Thank You, Father, that the veil has been torn, and I have this privilege to be in Your Presence as Moses was with You in the Most Holy Place. When I come boldly before You and lift my prayers to You, You listen! You care. My prayers are a sweet aroma to You. Gratitude fills my heart that You, the God of the Universe, Creator of all things, rejoice over me, delight in me, desire to meet with me. You know the cry of my heart. Hold me close, Lord. Keep my heart pure. Ready me for that day ... that glorious day when I shall stand before You in heaven and see You face to face. Oh what a joyous day that will be. I will kneel at Your feet and worship You forever!

I love You, Lord, and ask all this in Jesus' magnificent and powerful name. Amen.

NOTES

IN CASE YOU WERE WONDERING

Sometimes there is more to understanding Scripture than originally meets the eye. That's why our team wanted to provide you with additional information on some of the most popular verses from Exodus.

01.
JOY WILLIAMS

"And the angel of the Lord appeared to him in a flame of fire out of the midst of a bush. He looked, and behold, the bush was burning, yet it was not consumed" (Exodus 3:2).

The bush burning, yet not consumed, is the attention-getter in this verse. But the One appearing in the bush deserves our attention the most. *"The angel of the Lord"* might sound like an angel as a created being. However, in Exodus 3:6, when the Lord saw He had Moses' attention, *"He said, 'I am the God of your father ...' And Moses hid his face, for he was afraid to look upon God."*

Clearly, the One in the bush was the Creator, not the created. In addition, most Bible scholars therefore see *"the angel of the Lord"* as being God the Son, Jesus Christ. For *"No one has ever seen God; the only God, who is at the Father's side, he has made him known"* (John 1:18).

This foreshadowing of Christ's incarnation in this passage is a revelation of His being with us before the *"fullness of time"* (see Galatians 4:4). As the Savior who delivered humanity from the bondage of sin, He also through Moses delivered Israel from their bondage in Egypt. (Jude 5)

02.
QUANTRILLA ARD

"Then the Lord said, 'I have surely seen the affliction of my people who are in Egypt and have heard their cry because of their taskmasters. I know their sufferings'" (Exodus 3:7).

Have you ever been through something so painful you didn't have the strength to speak? And the only communication you could muster were hot, stinging tears? I can only imagine the children of Israel in Egypt, burdened, broken and crying out for deliverance. Here's what's special about this verse. In the middle of their pain, God told Moses that He saw and heard them. The Lord moved to act on their behalf not just because of His compassion, but also because He *knew* their suffering. Like the children of Israel stuck in their physical bondage, we may, at times, feel God has forgotten us, that He has not seen nor heard our cries of suffering. When those feelings arise, we can look back to this verse and know that God has heard and seen and knows our pain, and He is working on our deliverance from spiritual bondage. God doesn't just speak to our pain, He steps into it with us because He is acquainted with it. (Isaiah 53:3) Sometimes He will deliver us from our pain, and sometimes He will deliver us through it.

03.
BETHANY RUTH

"God said to Moses, 'I AM WHO I AM.' And he said, 'Say this to the people of Israel: I AM has sent me to you'" (Exodus 3:14).

"I AM WHO I AM" is translated from the Hebrew phrase "ehyeh asher ehyeh." Our infinite, eternal God reminded the Jews, and us, of His absolute, unchanging existence with the words *"I AM."* In addition, God revealed to Moses His personal, proper name YHWH, which is transliterated *Yahweh* in English, called the Tetragrammaton by scholars and used interchangeably with *"I AM"* in these verses. In our English Bible translations, we may miss something of great significance regarding this name of God. In Jewish tradition, *Yahweh* was too sacred to utter out loud. Instead, the Jews substituted the name *Adonai,* which means "My Lord" — His title, in place of His name. Our English translations continue this tradition today. When you see *"The Lord"* with capital letters, you will know the original manuscripts used the name "Yahweh." Let us not be afraid to call on God's name because He desires an intimate relationship with His people. (Isaiah 52:6)

04.
BETHANY RUTH

"And the Lord went before them by day in a pillar of cloud to lead them along the way, and by night in a pillar of fire to give them light, that they might travel by day and by night. The pillar of cloud by day and the pillar of fire by night did not depart from before the people" (Exodus 13:21-22).

God graciously gave the Israelites a visual manifestation of His presence to guide them as they departed from Egypt. God's presence in the pillar led the Israelites away from possible war early in their travels by taking them a longer way around, through the desert. (Exodus 13:17-18) The fire provided light in the darkness, (Exodus 13:21) and the cloud likely allowed protection from the heat of the desert during the day. God's presence in the pillar defended them from danger when the Egyptians caught up with them. (Exodus 14:19-20) The cloud indicated when the Israelites were to camp and when they were to move on and the Israelites never set out until the pillar moved. Later in the Israelites' journey, God's presence in the cloud covered and filled the tabernacle. (Exodus 40:34) God faithfully shepherded the Israelites over many years. (Numbers 9:15-22) What a remarkable picture of God's care over His people.

05.
ERIC GAGNON

"There the LORD made for them a statute and a rule, and there he tested them, saying, "If you will diligently listen to the voice of the LORD your God, and do that which is right in his eyes, and give ear to his commandments and keep all his statutes, I will put none of the diseases on you that I put on the Egyptians, for I am the LORD, your healer" (Exodus 15:25-26).

The diseases "put on the Egyptians" refers to the plagues that God had just sent, particularly the plague of making water undrinkable, and which God reverses at Marah, making the bitter water sweet. (Exodus 15:22-25) In the very next verses, the Israelites grumble against Aaron and Moses, which is certainly not "doing right" in God's eyes, and as we read the rest of Exodus (and the rest of the Bible) we see the point of this test: 1) to show our need for God our Savior, 2) to reveal God in Christ as our Healer, and 3) to teach us obedience. Since the Israelites continued to fail this test, they learned (and also show us) that no one "does right" all of the time according to God's holy standard. *"Surely there is not a righteous man on earth who does good and never sins"* (Ecclesiastes 7:20). They also learn, again and again, that God is the healer and their source of all healing. This verse isn't saying that if we trust in God, we will never get sick, or that if we get sick, that God guarantees our healing. Rather, it points us to the God-man who came healing the sick, proving that Jesus Himself is God-the-Healer. Some of our diseases will not be healed until the resurrection, but they will all be healed! Until then, as with the Israelites, God may use hardship to train us in righteousness. (Hebrews 12:7-11)

06.
JOY WILLIAMS

"You shall have no other gods before me" (Exodus 20:3).

This is the first of the Ten Commandments God gave to Israel as they assembled at the foot of Mount Sinai. At first glance, we might think God is only referring to physical idols. If we worship any object as a god, it is an offense to God's holiness, faithfulness and love.

Sadly, the Old Testament contains several examples of Israel how veered from God's directive by worshiping the gods of Egypt where they were once captive and the gods of neighboring nations where they lived. But the idolatry didn't end there.

When God told the Israelites to *"have no other gods before me,"* He also meant to have no other gods *besides me*. In Matthew 22:36-38, Jesus said, *"You shall love the Lord your God with all your heart and with all your soul and with all your mind. This is the great and first commandment."* Whatever or whomever we love, fear, serve, delight in or depend on more than God keeps us from giving our "all" to Him. Therefore, Exodus 20:3 instructs us to keep God first and to worship Him only.

07.
BETHANY RUTH

"You shall not make for yourself a carved image, or any likeness of anything that is in heaven above, or that is in the earth beneath, or that is in the water under the earth" (Exodus 20:4).

The Israelites lived among nations that worshipped tangible images of their gods, called idols. The gods of Egypt included the sun, moon and stars from *"heaven above,"* oxen, sheep, cats and dogs from *"the earth beneath"* and crocodiles and fish from *"the water"* (Exodus 20:4). In this commandment, God prohibits not only making images for worshipping the gods of other nations, but making any image in an attempt to represent the Creator, the One True God. Anything cut from wood or stone, any metal melted or formed, anything created by man can never represent our Lord, our Almighty Jehovah, and will quickly become an idol, even if that was not the original intent. Jesus explained this further when He said, *"God is spirit, and those who worship him must worship in spirit and truth"* (John 4:24). Bowing down or worshipping any created image is not worshipping the One True God.

08.
BRONWYN CARDWELL

"Remember the Sabbath day, to keep it holy" (Exodus 20:8).

The fourth commandment was a command that God's people remember to keep the seventh day of the week sacred to the Lord. The word "holy" means "set apart for a special purpose." The Sabbath was to be set apart and hallowed. Further instructions were given in the following two verses: Man was to pursue his own work for six days, but on the seventh day, he was to rest even as God rested on the seventh day of creation. (Exodus 20:9-10) The Lord's heart for His Sabbath was also revealed through His words to the prophet Isaiah: *"If, because of the Sabbath, you restrain your foot from doing as you wish on My holy day, and call the Sabbath a pleasure, and the holy day of the LORD honorable, and honor it, desisting from your own ways, from seeking your own pleasure and speaking your own word, then you will take delight in the LORD, and I will make you ride on the heights of the earth; and I will feed you with the heritage of Jacob your father, for the mouth of the LORD has spoken"* (Isaiah 58:13).

09.
MARISSA HENLEY

"Honor your father and your mother, that your days may be long in the land that the Lord your God is giving you" (Exodus 20:12).

Honoring our parents might seem like a minor issue compared to murder and adultery, and yet God singled out this commandment as the only one with a promise attached. (See Deuteronomy 5:16 and Ephesians 6:1-3.) God gave this command to ensure care for the elderly, and He also gives it as a provision for our own rebellious hearts. God has given us the family unit as a training ground: As we learn to honor and obey our parents, we learn to submit to the other authority structures the Lord has put in place. Our obedience to our parents prepares us for obedience to our heavenly Father who has lovingly adopted us as His sons and daughters in Jesus Christ.

10.
MELANIE PORTER

"The LORD passed before him and proclaimed, 'The LORD, the LORD, a God merciful and gracious, slow to anger, and abounding in steadfast love and faithfulness, keeping steadfast love for thousands, forgiving iniquity and transgression and sin, but who will by no means clear the guilty, visiting the iniquity of the fathers on the children and the children's children, to the third and the fourth generation'" (Exodus 34:6-7).

These two verses give us a transparent view into the character of God. The Lord, Himself, is describing His personality, righteousness and spiritual integrity to Moses. In the Jewish culture, these descriptive words are known as part of the "Thirteen Attributes" and are still recited in Synagogues today. Merciful, slow to anger, abounding in steadfast love, and gracious are words with meanings that capture the very essence of God. The nature of "merciful" portrays active, unending compassion. Scholar F.B. Meyer wrote that the word means "tenderly pitiful." The cultural meaning behind "graciousness" originates from the ideal to bend or stoop down in kindness to an inferior. The Jewish Study Bible says, "keeping steadfast love for thousands"; means "locking up grace." It carries a connotation of "to lock or preserve," which translates to God preserving His covenant love for us.

END NOTES

INTRO CONTENT

[1] Hill, Andrew E. and John H. Walton. A Survey of the Old Testament, 2nd Edition. Grand Rapids, MI: Zondervan, 1991, 2000. p. 83.

[2] House, Paul R. and Eric Mitchell. Old Testament Survey, 2nd Edition. Nashville, TN: B&H Publishing Group, 2007. p. 46.

[3] Currid, John D. Exodus. ESV Archaeology Study Bible. Wheaton, IL: Crossway, 2017. p. 92

[4] Currid, John D. Exodus. ESV Archaeology Study Bible. Wheaton, IL: Crossway, 2017. p.88.

[5] Beale, G.K. and Mitchell Kim. God Dwells Among Us: Expanding Eden to the Ends of the Earth. Downers Grove, IL: IVP Books, 2014. p. 29.

[6] Harris, Kenneth Laing. Exodus. The ESV Study Bible. Wheaton, IL: Crossway, 2008. p. 142.

[7] Horton, Michael on G.K. Beale's God Dwells Among Us. Back cover and intro page content

WEEK 1

DAY 1
[1] Wiersbe, Warren W. BE Delivered: Finding Freedom By Following God. OT Commentary Exodus. Colorado Springs, CO: David C. Cook, 1998. p.23.

[2] Cole, R. Alan. Exodus: An Introduction and Commentary. Downers Grove, IL: Inter-Varsity Press, 1977. p.71

DAY 2
[3] Oswalt, John N. Exodus. Cornerstone Biblical Commentary, Volume 1, edited by Philip W. Comfort. Carol Stream, IL: Tyndale, 2008. p. 303

DAY 3
[4] Merida, Tony. Exalting Jesus in Exodus. Christ-Centered Exposition, edited by David Platt, Daniel L. Akin, and Tony Merida. Nashville, TN: Holman, 2014. p. 26.

DAY 4
[5] Stuart, Douglas K. Exodus. The New American Commentary, Vol. 2. Nashville, TN: B&H Publishing Group, 2006. p. 103.

[6] Oswalt, John N. Exodus. Cornerstone Biblical Commentary, Volume 1, edited by Philip W. Comfort. Carol Stream, IL: Tyndale, 2008. p. 304

Day 5
[7] Enns, Peter. Exodus. The NIV Application Commentary. Grand Rapids, MI: Zondervan, 2000. p. 110.

[8] Enns, Peter. Exodus. The NIV Application Commentary. Grand Rapids, MI: Zondervan, 2000. p. 110.

[9] Enns, Peter. Exodus. The NIV Application Commentary. Grand Rapids, MI: Zondervan, 2000. p. 110.

WEEK 2

DAY 6
[1] Enns, Peter. Exodus. The NIV Application Commentary. Grand Rapids, MI: Zonderan, 2000. pp. 110–111

[2] Enns, Peter. Exodus. The NIV Application Commentary. Grand Rapids, MI: Zondervan, 2000. p. 110.

DAY 7
[3] Kaiser, W. C., Jr. Exodus. In F. E. Gaebelein (Ed.), The Expositor's Bible Commentary: Genesis, Exodus, Leviticus, Numbers Grand Rapids, MI: Zondervan, 1990. Vol. 2, pp. 331–332.

[4] Stuart, Douglas K. Exodus. The New American Commentary, Vol. 2. Nashville, TN: B&H Publishing Group, 2006. p.146

[5] Enns, Peter. Exodus. The NIV Application Commentary. Grand Rapids, MI: Zondervan, 2000. p. 136

DAY 8
[6] Stuart, Douglas K. Exodus. The New American Commentary, Vol. 2. Nashville, TN: B&H Publishing Group, 2006. p.159

[7] Blue Letter Bible. Strong's Hebrew Lexicon (ESV) Web. 4 Sep, 2020. <https://www.blueletterbible.org//lang/lexicon/lexicon.cfm?Strongs=H3045&t=ESV>

[8] Enns, Peter. Exodus. The NIV Application Commentary. Grand Rapids, MI: Zondervan, 2000. pp. 161-163.

DAY 9
[9] Stuart, Douglas K. Exodus. The New American Commentary, Vol. 2. Nashville, TN: B&H Publishing Group, 2006. p. 162

[10] Kaiser, W. C., Jr. Exodus. In F. E. Gaebelein (Ed.), The Expositor's Bible Commentary: Genesis, Exodus, Leviticus, Numbers Grand Rapids, MI: Zondervan, 1990. Vol. 2, pp. 337).

[11] Stuart, Douglas K. Exodus. The New American Commentary, Vol. 2. Nashville, TN: B&H Publishing Group, 2006. p.164

DAY 10
[12] Kaiser, W. C., Jr. Exodus. In F. E. Gaebelein (Ed.), The Expositor's Bible Commentary: Genesis, Exodus, Leviticus, Numbers Grand Rapids, MI: Zondervan, 1990. Vol. 2, p. 339

[13] Stuart, Douglas K. Exodus. The New American Commentary, Vol. 2. Nashville, TN: B&H Publishing Group, 2006. pp. 169–170

[14] Blue Letter Bible. Strong's Hebrew Lexicon (ESV). Web. 8 Sep, 2020. <https://www.blueletterbible.org//lang/lexicon/lexicon.cfm?Strongs=H7115&t=ESV>.

WEEK 3

DAY 11
[1] Stuart, Douglas K. Exodus. The New American Commentary, Vol. 2. Nashville, TN: B&H Publishing Group, 2006. pp. 175–176

[2] Stuart, Douglas K. Exodus. The New American Commentary, Vol. 2. Nashville, TN: B&H Publishing Group, 2006. p. 179

DAY 12
[3] Stuart, Douglas K. Exodus. The New American Commentary, Vol. 2. Nashville, TN: B&H Publishing Group, 2006. p. 195

[4] Enns, Peter. Exodus. The NIV Application Commentary. Grand Rapids, MI: Zondervan, 2000. p. 196

[5] Calvin, Four Last Books of Moses, pp. 112–13.

DAY 13
[6] Enns, Peter. Exodus. The NIV Application Commentary. Grand Rapids, MI: Zondervan, 2000. p. 200).

[7] Enns, Peter. Exodus. The NIV Application Commentary. Grand Rapids, MI: Zondervan, 2000. p. 208

DAY 14
[8] Stuart, Douglas K. Exodus. The New American Commentary, Vol. 2. Nashville, TN: B&H Publishing Group, 2006. p. 222

[9] Enns, Peter. Exodus. The NIV Application Commentary. Grand Rapids, MI: Zondervan, 2000. p. 226).

DAY 15
[10] Stuart, Douglas K. Exodus. The New American Commentary, Vol. 2. Nashville, TN: B&H Publishing Group, 2006. p. 255

[11] Enns, Peter. Exodus. The NIV Application Commentary. Grand Rapids, MI: Zondervan, 2000. pp. 228–229

WEEK 4

DAY 16
[1] Carson, D. A. "The Ground of All Human Assurance Before God." www.thegospelcoalition,org/artic/the-ground-of-all-human-assurance-before-god. 27 January 2016. Accessed 11 September 2020.

[2] Ryken, Leland; Wilhoit, James; Longman III, Tremper. Dictionary of Biblical Knowledge. Inter-Varsity Press, England, 1998. p. 498.

DAY 17
[3] Ryken, Leland; Wilhoit, James; Longman III, Tremper. Dictionary of Biblical Knowledge. Inter-Varsity Press, England, 1998, p. 758.

[4] Spurgeon, Charles, "Christ Our Passover." www.spurgeon.org/resource-library/sermons/christ-our-passover, 2 December 1855, New Park Street Volume 2. Accessed 11 September 2020.

DAY 19
[5] Spurgeon, Charles. "Marah, or The Bitter Waters Sweetened." www.spurgeon.org/resource-library/sermons/marah-or-the-bitter-waters-sweetened, 23 April 1871. Metropolitan Tabernacle Pulpit Volume 17. Accessed 11 September /2020.

DAY 20
[6] Wesley, John. "Wesley's Explanatory Notes." www.biblestudytools.com/commentaries/Wesley-explanatory-notes/exodus-16, verse 16:3, Accessed 11 September 2020.

[7] Wesley, John. "Wesley's Explanatory Notes." www.biblestudytools.com/commentaries/Wesley-explanatory-notes/exodus -17, verse 17:5, Accessed 9 September 2020.

WEEK 5

DAY 21
[1] Henry, Matthew. "Matthew Henry Commentary on the Whole Bible." www.biblestudytools.com/commentaries/matthew-henry-complete/exodus/17. Verses 8-16. Accessed 9 September 2020.

[2] Calvin, John. Calvin's Commentary on the Bible. www.studylight.org/commentaries/cal/exodus-18. Verse 23. Accessed 9 September 2020.

DAY 22
[3] Wesley, John. "Wesley's Explanatory Notes." www.biblestudytools.com/commentaries/wesleys-explanatory-notes/exodus/exodus-19. Verse 19:6. Accessed 11 September 2020.

DAY 23
[4] Wesley, John. "Wesley's Explanatory Notes." www.biblestudytools.com/commentaries/wesleys-explanatory-notes/exodus/exodus-20. Verse 19:16. Accessed 11 September 2020.

DAY 24
[5] Goodrick, Edward W. and Kohlenberger, John R., III. "The Strongest NIV Exhaustive Concordance." Zondervan, 1990. p.1419 (Hebrew to English dictionary words #3707, #3711).

[6]Goodrick, Edward W. and Kohlenberger, John R., III. "The Strongest NIV Exhaustive Concordance." Zondervan, 1990. p.1419 (Hebrew to English dictionary words #3707, #3711).

WEEKEND REFLECTION
[7] Newton, John. "The Baptist Hymnal." No. 330.

WEEK 6

DAY 26
[1] Ryken, Philip Graham and Hughes, R. Kent. Exodus: Saved for God's Glory. Wheaton, IL: Crossway Books, 2005. p. 783.
[2] Motyer, J. Alec. The Message of Exodus: The Days of Our Pilgrimage.

Nottingham, England: Inter-Varsity Press, 2005. p. 249.

DAY 28
[3] Mackay, John L. Exodus. Mentor Commentaries. Fearn, Ross-shire, Great Britain: Mentor, 2001. p. 525.
[4] Ryken, Philip Graham and Hughes, R. Kent. Exodus: Saved for God's Glory. Wheaton, IL: Crossway Books, 2005. p. 978.

DAY 29
[5] Mackay, John L. Exodus. Mentor Commentaries. Fearn, Ross-shire, Great Britain: Mentor, 2001. p. 538.

DAY 30
[6] Ryken, Philip Graham and Hughes, R. Kent. Exodus: Saved for God's Glory. Wheaton, IL: Crossway Books, 2005. p. 1022.

WEEK 7

DAY 31
[1] Ryken, Philip Graham and Hughes, R. Kent. Exodus: Saved for God's Glory. Wheaton, IL: Crossway Books, 2005. p. 1071.
[2] Ryken, Philip Graham and Hughes, R. Kent. Exodus: Saved for God's Glory. Wheaton, IL: Crossway Books, 2005. p. 1071.

DAY 33
[3] Motyer, J. Alec. The Message of Exodus: The Days of Our Pilgrimage. Nottingham, England: Inter-Varsity Press, 2005. p. 318.

[4] Bruce, Barbara J. "Sabbath." Ed. Chad Brand et al. Holman Illustrated Bible Dictionary. Nashville, TN: B&H, 2015. p. 1396.

DAY 35
[5] Ryken, Philip Graham and Hughes, R. Kent. Exodus: Saved for God's Glory. Wheaton, IL: Crossway Books, 2005. p. 1091.

[6] Crossway Bibles. The ESV Study Bible. Wheaton, IL: Crossway Bibles. p. 196. (Note on Exodus 31:3)

THE TABERNACLE AS A SYMBOL OF THE COSMOS
[1] Fowler, M. D. (1992). Incense Altars. In D. N. Freedman (Ed.), The Anchor Yale Bible Dictionary (Vol. 3, p. 409). New York: Doubleday.

About Proverbs 31 Ministries

She is clothed with strength and dignity;
she can laugh at the days to come.

PROVERBS 31:25

Proverbs 31 Ministries is a nondenominational, nonprofit Christian ministry that seeks to lead women into a personal relationship with Christ. With Proverbs 31:10-31 as a guide, Proverbs 31 Ministries reaches women in the middle of their busy days through free devotions, podcast episodes, speaking events, conferences, resources, online Bible studies and training in the call to write, speak and lead others.

We are real women offering real-life solutions to those striving to maintain life's balance, in spite of today's hectic pace and cultural pull away from godly principles.

Wherever a woman may be on her spiritual journey, Proverbs 31 Ministries exists to be a trusted friend who understands the challenges she faces and walks by her side, encouraging her as she walks toward the heart of God.

Visit us online today at proverbs31.org!

LOOKING FOR YOUR NEXT STUDY?

JOIN US FOR:

When I Don't Know What To Believe

Why Jesus Is the Answer

A HEBREWS STUDY GUIDE

ORDER THE STUDY GUIDE

AVAILABLE MAY 2021 AT p31boookstore.com

FOLLOW ALONG IN THE FIRST 5 MOBILE APP